Privileged Thinking in Today's Schools

The Implications for Social Justice

David Barnett, Carol Christian,
Richard Hughes, Rocky Wallace

*Foundation and Graduate Studies in Education
Graduate School of Education
Morehead State University*

ROWMAN & LITTLEFIELD EDUCATION

A division of

ROWMAN & LITTLEFIELD PUBLISHERS, INC.
Lanham • New York • Toronto • Plymouth, UK

Published by Rowman & Littlefield Education
A division of Rowman & Littlefield Publishers, Inc.
A wholly owned subsidiary of The Rowman & Littlefield Publishing Group, Inc.
4501 Forbes Boulevard, Suite 200, Lanham, Maryland 20706
http://www.rowmaneducation.com

Estover Road
Plymouth PL6 7PY
United Kingdom

The Poem "A Prayer for Children" by Ina Hughs is reprinted with permission from her book *A Prayer for Children*.

British Library Cataloguing in Publication Information Available

Library of Congress Cataloging-in-Publication Data

Privileged thinking in today's schools : the implications for social justice / David Barnett ... [et al.].
    p. cm.
  Includes bibliographical references.
   ISBN 978-1-60709-969-7 (cloth : alk. paper) — ISBN 978-1-60709-970-3 (pbk. : alk. paper) — ISBN 978-1-60709-971-0 (electronic)
   1. Educational equalization—United States   2. Children with social disabilities—Education—United States. 3. Social justice—United States.   I. Barnett, David, 1954-
   LC213.2.P75 2010
   379.2'60973—dc22   2010028876

Printed in the United States of America

♾ ™ The paper used in this publication meets the minimum requirements of American National Standard for Information Sciences—Permanence of Paper for Printed Library Materials, ANSI/NISO Z39.48-1992.

Dedication

This book is dedicated to the students and their parents whom we remember as somehow not receiving the same breaks others were given. When we reflect on our years down in the trenches while serving in school leadership roles, and all the good work that was done, we also recall that sometimes, usually because we didn't know any better, we allowed local customs, practices, and the status quo to rule to the extent that social injustice was actually—albeit inadvertently and unintentionally—promoted. With this project, we hope to help future generations of educators to be more sensitive to issues that we, quite frankly, missed in the past. By opening their eyes, perhaps they will be better equipped to help students and staff in the public school environment and to lead as we wish we had.

Contents

Preface

When first discussing the possibility of working together on a collaborative effort to address how privileged thinking can result in social injustice, we, the four authors, were reminded of so many examples from our own experiences in school work that the opportunity to shed more light on the subject was too great to ignore. Thus, this project is not so much an indictment of what is still not working in schools, but a confession of what we knowingly or unwittingly did wrong, largely because we may have followed the paths of least resistance and too readily blended into the landscape of our culture as a whole.

If those leading classrooms, schools, and districts are truly committed to moving from good to great, then taking an honest look inside the customs and daily practices of the educational system is essential. And if social injustice is to be fairly addressed, then we must take a closer look through the eyes of the victims—those "others" who do not remember school being the pleasant and fulfilling place it was for us and our children.

Take a deep breath and join us here! You might be surprised to learn of issues that you, too, have taken for granted, and that, upon reflection, may have resulted in something less than your best work. And you might be set free (and better prepared) to address any hint of injustice—regardless of the number of students it impacts—that will intermittently surface in your school community.

Acknowledgments

We are eternally grateful to our families, who by always being there continuously encourage us to keep teaching, writing, and making a difference so that we can stand in the gap for our students, and enable them to achieve their potential to make an enormously positive difference in the schools, communities, and world they serve.

Chapter 1

Don't Give Me Justice

Deep-thinking, educated people in America really do not want justice, do they? Since justice implies fairness and one getting what he or she deserves, many (perhaps most) are not conditioned to desire such, are they? Think about it. You are driving fifty-five miles per hour in a thirty-five-mile-per-hour speed zone, are stopped, issued a ticket, later given a court date, and what do you do before the ink completely dries on the ticket? You, of course, begin thinking, "How do I get out of this? Who can contact the judge and get this forgiven?" This is particularly true if you have previously been charged with speeding and had points deducted from your driver's license record! And if educated teachers, coaches, principals, or superintendents in the American education arena do not want justice—but something better—for themselves, do they also really want it for their students . . . for all their students?

Actually, what individuals want in the above referenced traffic scenario is at least mercy and at best grace! Mercy, if granted, would ensure that they not get what they deserve—a permanent court record of the offense and the payment of a traffic fine, or maybe even traffic school (perish the thought, particularly with their busy schedules!). Grace—and this is what they would really prefer—would give them more than they deserve (no traffic fine, no traffic school, and the judge modifying the charge from speeding to "faulty equipment!").

Were *privileged thinking* and *social injustice* just defined? And if so, would those (most, if not all) educated Americans serving throughout this country as teachers, principals, superintendents, coaches, directors of musical groups, leaders of various extracurricular programs, and board of education members really suffer knowingly or unwittingly, from such "abnormalities"? Would a

1

side effect of these ailments render these leaders in the education arena seemingly incapable of guaranteeing to *all* their students social justice and an avoidance of privileged thinking that would do them harm? And if such maladies exist in the lives of those who lead America, those who lead the profession (education) from which all other professions emanate, can they be cured?

Can the winners (those students in our schools benefiting from privileged thinking, and concomitantly receiving social justice) and the losers (those students in our schools negatively impacted from privileged thinking and, subsequently, social injustice) be identified? And more importantly, can the educational leaders be healed of this malaise so that a decade from now America's schools can be largely free of privileged thinking and social injustice and their harmful effects on students?

To equip one to better understand the questions raised above, explore a couple of examples of how privileged thinking—which more often than not has become ingrained in the culture, and subsequently, and unwittingly, into the thinking process of many educational leaders—leads to social injustice for the students they serve.

Social justice demands that *all* students have teachers best suited for them. Conventional wisdom, if informed and directed by social justice, would demand that the students who have the greatest educational needs—the hardest to teach, those coming from the inner cities or the lowest economic segments of the counties, those coming from broken homes, single-parent homes, or from orphan or foster homes—would be assigned the best teachers in the school (those teachers with experience, confidence, an indomitable spirit, a passion for their work, excellent classroom management skills, and an expectation that *all* students will succeed). Yet, in reality, this rarely occurs, as privileged thinking on the part of school leaders trumps social justice and conventional wisdom!

After all, should not those students to whom schools don't make much difference anyway—the top 25 percent of the academically talented, not the difficult to teach—be assigned the least competent, least experienced teachers who do not possess all the favorable characteristics previously mentioned? Say that again! Schools don't make that much of a difference for whom? Researchers such as James Coleman (1966), Robert Marzano (2003), and Caroline Hoxby (2003) have concluded that, for students from middle/high socioeconomic status (SES) and high family support/involvement backgrounds, 80 to 93 percent of the variance in their standardized tests scores is not attributable to the schools they attend, or the staff to which they are assigned, but rather the background from which they come!

But, look out! Here comes privileged thinking, even if it is subconsciously ingrained in the minds of the decision makers. The students who would do nearly as well with beginning, less experienced, less competent teachers (the students whose parents are the doctors, lawyers, corporate leaders, community leaders, and movers and shakers) are assigned the best teachers, and the others (the down-and-out kids, the low-achieving minorities, the Hispanics, those from the wrong side of the track) to the worst teachers . . . and this is not to assail those teachers, but to make a valid, well-known point.

Why is there not a revolt by the highly competent, experienced teachers whose intuition (conventional wisdom) and training dictate that they should be teaching the most challenging students? Why are they not lined up at the principal's door demanding that staff assignments be changed to reflect social justice? Could it be that they too are victims of privileged thinking? Were they not improperly assigned when they began teaching? Have they not paid the price? Do they not now deserve to teach the brightest and best-prepared students?

In probing prevalent practice further, is the high school master class schedule an aspect of the school where *all* students can expect and receive social justice? Is there anything more important than the appropriate distribution of classes and assignment of staff? Well, in building the schedule, where do school administrators start? Is it not with those so called singletons, or doubletons, to which the top 25 percent, or especially the top 10 percent are assigned? And what about those coaches? Do not they all—or most of them—need, even deserve, the last period of the day as a planning period? And if so assigned, surely they will plan their academic class pursuits, not go to the athletic arena and make preparations for practice! As one knows, they are hired to be teachers first, then coaches! Aren't they?

What about the head of the math department who has had planning first period for 10 years, loves to teach technology classes at least two periods per day, even though two other staff members could teach those classes, and she could serve best by teaching (accepting) two pre-algebra classes? And what happens when there are seemingly irresolvable conflicts in the master schedule? Do these conflicts often involve students from the bottom 75 percent or bottom 50 percent academic achievers? And is it their parents who storm into the principal's office demanding a change? Or are perceived conflicts pointed out by the parents of the top 25 percent academic achievers, the high SES parents, maybe the ones serving on the site-based decision-making council, vociferously demanding a change in the schedule? Are those changes often made?

If justice is defined as a setting where all people are treated equally and get what they deserve, then social justice could be defined with examples of these phenomena occurring in social contexts (the schools for the purpose of this book). It follows that the antithesis of social justice would be social injustice—people (students) being treated unequally and not getting what they deserve.

If the word *privileged* implies the receiving of an act, service, or material good based upon perceived differences—and it does—then privileged thinking must be a biased human thought process, even if it occurs below the level of consciousness and to the extent that it becomes habitual, learned, perfunctory, calloused, routine, involuntary, and automatic—and is accompanied with a positive, or favored, result for its recipients. Its antithesis would be unprivileged thinking, bearing the same descriptors with the exception of its effect on recipients who receive a negative, unfavorable result.

To illustrate that well-intentioned people who fill leadership roles in American schools are prone to consciously or unconsciously want for themselves—because of privileged thinking—something other than (even better than) justice under the law, revisit the scenario regarding the issuance of a speeding ticket. If one does not expect justice under the law, does not want to pay a fine, and may even want the record expunged (or to reflect something other than what actually happened), it is certainly plausible that he or she is capable of routinely practicing privileged thinking, which results in social injustice for an unacceptably high number of students in America's schools.

If a corollary of privileged thinking is social injustice, and it likely is, then the exoneration of those guilty of traffic violations could, and likely would, result in a tax increase for everyone (for example, as municipalities build into their budgets the receipt of traffic fines). Now, maybe one ought to quit preaching and go to meddling. Across this country it is commonplace to use property taxes to finance schools.

It is almost as common for government officials, school board members, school administrators, and many citizens to allow—even expect—property value administrators (PVAs) to undervalue the homes (property) of innumerable privileged thinkers (many of whom specifically request such a devaluation in order to lower their school taxes). What is the corollary here? Isn't it less money for schools, a social injustice, particularly against low SES, unrepresented students? And aren't those participating in this travesty well-intentioned, law-abiding, churchgoing, highly respected, citizens of their communities?

Inherent within privileged thinking and its corollary, social injustice, are some very serious implications!

QUESTIONS FOR REFLECTION

1. Some individuals reading this chapter would be quick to say, "Why, I'd pay my fine. I would not even think about asking that it be forgiven!" Or, "I pay my taxes. I'd never ask the PVA for a break!" Maybe that is true,

but can you think of, and expound upon, a couple of other scenarios where good, well-intentioned people may be guilty of privileged thinking and social injustice?

2. Do you know of school officials (teachers, coaches, principals, superintendents) from whom you have seen acts of privileged thinking and social injustice, even though they would be quick to say that they would gladly and quickly pay for their traffic violation and taxes? Give a couple of examples.

3. Whether or not you are a school official, can you give a couple of examples of times when you may have practiced privileged thinking and social injustice?

4. Considering the math department head scenario, how would he or she explain it if asked why he or she clung to first period planning and teaching the technology courses when that may not be in the best interest of students? If you then explained the concepts of privileged thinking and social injustice, how do you think he or she would respond?

SUGGESTIONS FOR FURTHER READING:

Coleman, J. (1966). *The James Coleman Report.* Massachusetts: Harvard University.

Hoxby, C. (2003) *National School Board Meeting Presentation.* San Francisco.

Marzano, R. (2003) *What Works in Schools.* Alexandria, VA: Association for Supervision and Curriculum Development.

Chapter 2

How Much Money Does Daddy Make, Mommy?

When children are small, they often assume their friends and classmates are playing by the same rules. And they get along well, so inspiring to watch in their innocence. But one day, they realize that they come from different worlds, based on the income and social status of their parents. And thus, a natural separation begins to take place, as the "haves" and the "have nots" withdraw to hang out with their own kind.

"This school does not discriminate on the basis of race, creed, gender, or socioeconomic status." School Announcement:

Cheerleading tryouts will be held on Thursday, September 25. Prior to tryouts there will be one full week of open gym practice sessions. Anyone interested is encouraged to try out. The minimal gymnastic skills required for tryouts are roundoff back handspring, front flip, roundoff back handspring/backflip, and aerial cartwheel. Dance experience is required.

The announcement should have read:

Cheerleading tryouts will be held on Thursday, September 25. Prior to tryouts there will be one week of open gym practices sessions. Anyone with less than three years of gymnastic/dance experience need not try out. The minimal combined family income for cheerleaders is $80,000 in order for candidates to be able to pay for the uniforms, camps, and private lessons. Those interested must have a stay-at-home mom available to shuttle cheerleaders to and from practice, camps, gymnastic and dance lessons, games, and competitions.

Is this tryout really open to anyone interested? Perhaps it is open to anyone interested who has invested in and can afford at least three years of expensive gymnastics prior to tryouts. The cost to be a cheerleader today is astronomical when considering the expense of private gymnastic and dance lessons, participation in summer cheerleading camps, four to six different uniforms with matching hair ribbons, tennis shoes, and pom-poms. In addition, there is the cost of taking cheerleaders to and from all events.

What about bands? Athletic teams? Are they really open to all, or only to the privileged few who can afford private lessons, summer camps, and instruments?

Now that we have your attention, we are not advocating eliminating any of these competitive activities in schools. But how can we better prepare more kids to be competitive at tryout time? How can we involve more kids in extracurricular activities? Here are a few suggestions. See how many more your staff can generate, and then actively look for ways to make them happen.

- Offer year-round after-school cheerleading clinics.
- Develop a high-quality after-school intramural program (table tennis, badminton, basketball, bowling, golf, etc.).
- Offer dance clinics after school.
- Develop a competitive cheerleading program that is a sport in and of itself. In addition, develop a cheerleading squad that focuses on leading cheers.
- Offer a music class where instruments are available, and any student can sign up. Have students rotate to the various instruments as needed.

QUESTIONS FOR REFLECTION

1. Have you ever looked at or logged the average yearly cost for cheerleading, being in a band, or playing a school sport?
2. What can we do to level the opportunity playing field?
3. Have you ever conducted a study on the family income status of students trying out for cheerleading, or playing in a band or sport teams? We may think that students choose to not try out for extracurricular groups when, in fact, participation is too expensive for lower-income families, therefore creating an elitist activity.
4. Have you ever looked at what the research says about students who are involved in extracurricular activities in regard to grades, attendance, and behavior in school? Involved kids feel connected to their school. Kids who participate have better attendance, lower dropout rates, higher grades, and higher test scores.

SUGGESTIONS FOR FURTHER READING:

Payne, R. (1996). *Framework for Understanding Poverty.* Highlands, TX: Aha Process Inc.

Edmonds, R. R. (1979). Some Schools Work and More Can. *Social Policy,* 9(5) (March–April), 29–32.

Chapter 3

The "N" Word

I've always wondered what it would be like to be white so I could wonder what it's like to be black.

Terrance moved down the hallway in his own distinctive way. It was something between a glide and a strut. Some kids thought it was cool, others thought it strange, and most others now didn't give Terrance a second thought. Basketball season had ended nearly a month ago as had the smiles and eye contact that had been a part of Terrance's life after a night of triple-doubles. All that talent exhibited during the basketball season almost elevated Terrance's status to a rock star. But now, few noticed him; most could care less.

Billy Joe was an exception. He noticed Terrance. He noticed the way he moved, the pick in his hair, and the baggy pants that rode about halfway down Terrance's rear end. Billy Joe also noticed that Terrance's status in the pecking order was lessening. Billy Joe knew about the pecking order. He'd spent much of his life looking up from near the bottom. Though Billy Joe's mother was a constant in his life, the men who frequented Billy Joe's home changed almost as often as Terrance was moved from one foster home to another. Billy Joe had learned to read his surroundings, and his surroundings were telling him that with just a little effort he could surpass Terrance's social status among his high school classmates.

"Hey, boy," Billy Joe sneered as Terrance passed by. "How many stations are you able to pull in with that thing sticking out of your hair?" Billy Joe laughed and elbowed his friends in an effort to gain their attention and respect. Terrance kept walking, either not hearing Billy Joe's comments or choosing to ignore them. "I'm talking to you, boy," Billy Joe shouted as Terrance rounded the corner and went out of sight. Billy Joe was starting to strut a bit himself, having elevated himself by making fun of Terrance, a fading star of the school.

The last period of the day found Terrance and Billy Joe both in biology class. While Billy Joe wondered if Terrance would be looking for him, he didn't dare show any type of care or concern. After all, pecking order and status were important and Billy Joe had scored some major points.

"Terrance," Ms. Tinsley asked, "Give me an example of something that has been changed as a result of photosynthesis." As a biology teacher, Ms. Tinsley always tried to connect the concepts she was teaching with the real world. She knew that this connection helped students learn, understand, and remember the concepts. There was no response from Terrance, so she asked again, "Terrance, think of something you saw on your way to school this morning that was changed by photosynthesis." Though Billy Joe couldn't answer the question either, he snickered and said to those near him, "Look at what a dumb ass Mr. Basketball really is."

The lesson wasn't lost on Ms. Tinsley either. She saw the tension and glares going back and forth between Billy Joe and Terrance. She made a mental note to watch both boys after class. She'd taught high school long enough to read the signs when students were about to settle an argument with their fists. But Ms. Tinsley also noticed something else. Now that basketball season had ended, Coach Blake never stopped by to see how Terrance was doing in class. All during the season Coach was there every Friday to check on his grades. If a major test was being planned, Coach Blake scheduled tutoring sessions and extra help for Terrance and any other players that might need some assistance. But now, it seemed that no one was giving Terrance much attention except Billy Joe, and that was about to take a predictable and unfortunate turn.

The next morning Billy Joe was starting to feel as if he wasn't on the bottom rung of the social ladder. Yesterday he'd been able to land some pretty solid verbal blows on Terrance without even a hint of retribution. Terrance moved past Billy Joe with his familiar low-rise jeans and black pick in his hair. "Hey, boy! Do you use that pick to scratch the cooties in your hair or did your momma forget to take it out after she dressed you this morning?" Billy Joe called. Again, Terrance kept moving as if Billy Joe's comments were meant for someone else. Little did Billy Joe know that the ambers in Terrance's gut were being stoked and were nearing the point of bursting. Billy Joe thought he'd landed another solid verbal blow and was feeling pretty good about himself. Every time he saw Terrance that day, Billy Joe would elbow his friends and snicker and shake his head. Moving up the social ladder was easier than Billy Joe thought it would be.

For several days Billy Joe kept up the verbal assault on Terrance. And every day Terrance moved past Billy Joe as if the words were spoken in a language that Terrance didn't understand. It was now Friday and Billy Joe wanted to cement his rising position on the social ladder before the dance that weekend. Just as Terrance had done every day for several days, with his drooping pants and familiar pick, he moved passed Billy Joe. Billy Joe was emboldened. "Hey, nigger . . ." The words were scarcely out of Billy Joe's mouth when Terrance turned, and with a pent-up frustration that suddenly exploded, he hit Billy Joe in the mouth with such force that Billy Joe's jaw bone was broken, and teeth fell to the floor. Billy Joe landed hard on the floor, out cold. Other students rushed to the scene hoping to see more action. But everything was over in less than ten seconds.

Seeing the students moving swiftly down the hallway, a couple of veteran teachers knew instinctively what was happening. Fights tend to cause a gathering and this one was no exception. Ms. Tinsley and Mr. Grout both got to the scene about the same time. While Mr. Grout tried to revive Billy Joe, Ms. Tinsley took Terrance to her office.

Though no one could know it at that time, Hamilton East High School, with its students, faculty, administration, and indeed the entire community, was getting ready to learn some difficult lessons concerning race relations. When race becomes a part of the mix many people do not make decisions based on fact. Sometimes in subtle ways and other times in ways that are more overt, prejudice and bias guide the thinking and decisions of what are usually well-reasoned people.

The impact that ethnicity and privileged thinking that is influenced by ethnicity have on a school setting cannot be ignored. Pretending bigotry doesn't exist doesn't change the fact that it does and is at work in every school in our nation. Think back to the infamous O.J. trial. On the day the verdict was announced we observed two reactions. One group of people was cheering while the other group stood in stunned disbelief. It wasn't O.J.'s guilt or innocence that caused this dichotomy. It was the color of his skin. Terrance and Billy Joe had different colored skin. As the school and larger community formed opinions about who was right and who was wrong, it was the color of their skin, not the facts of the case, that determined whose side one found him or herself in.

QUESTIONS FOR REFLECTION

1. What prejudices or biases do you have? Some may not be obvious. For example, do you assume that people from the Northeast talk fast and are difficult? Do you believe that people from the South are slow and dumb? Is the superintendent's child treated the same as the student who lives with

his grandmother who is in the early stages of Alzheimer's? What bias are you willing to admit? How does it impact your decisions?

2. During basketball season Coach Blake was always around checking on Terrance's grades. Following the season Coach wasn't concerned about Terrance's eligibility. What responsibility did the coach have toward Terrance and others on the team *after* the season ended? What policies or practices are in place in your school to help ensure student athlete success before, during, and after the season?

3. What steps could have been taken to help ensure this situation didn't occur? What was Ms. Tinsley's responsibility? How can the culture of the school make this type of situation either more or less frequent? What steps can school leaders take to alleviate this type of problem?

4. Hamilton East High School and the entire community nearly exploded because of the strong feelings this case generated. What steps should the school leaders take *before* a situation like this occurs?

5. Should Billy Joe and Terrance receive the same punishment? Why? Why not?

6. How can school leaders build alliances with groups of different ethnicities? Covey (2004) suggests that first we should seek to understand, then to be understood. How does the "n" word or other language meant to denigrate others make you feel when you hear it? Do you dismiss its explosive potential because you don't understand its impact on others? What is your "line in the sand" when it comes to jokes and small talk that tend to describe groups in negative, stereotypical ways?

SUGGESTIONS FOR FURTHER READING:

Asim, J. (2007). *The N word: Who can say it, who shouldn't, and why.* Boston: Houghton Mifflin.

Covey, S. (2004). *The 7 habits of highly effective people.* New York: Free Press.

Espinosa, L. (2004). Exploring race relations. Rethinking Schools Online, *18*(3). Available at http://www.rethinkingschools.org/archive/18_03/expl183.shtml.

Richeson, J., and Nussbaum, R. (2004). The impact of multiculturalism versus color-blindness on racial bias. *Journal of Experimental Social Psychology, 40*(3), 417–423.

Chapter 4

The "Back Hall" Kids

Who knows what they could have become, those "lost children" who didn't have an advocate in their corner. Too often, their teachers and principals—their lifelines—have looked the other way, not wanting to see the hollowness in their eyes . . . a hollowness that says, "I'm not going to grow up to be one of the lucky ones, am I? My life is going to be a long road. I know it. You know it. The other students know it. Let's not pretend anymore."

As a principal, Francis remembers caring for every child in the building. But he saw his main role as the shepherd of the staff. If he protected them, empowered and equipped them, helped build a culture that they enjoyed working in, then their energy and attitude in the classroom would benefit the kids in significant ways. But as he looks back, Francis realizes now that there were instances when students were drowning due to the "system" of school—the structure. He regrets that he didn't do more to challenge the traditional paradigms, as they from time to time raised their ugly heads and reeked of social injustice.

Francis remembers being a little puzzled that the parent boosters' elementary basketball league called the less experienced players their "B" squad. How could these well-intentioned dads know for sure who of these kids would develop and grow to be the varsity players at the high school several years down the road? After all, these were only fourth and fifth graders! But Francis let it ride. He now wonders how many of those little fellas bought into that label of "B" team, and never put on a uniform again after leaving elementary school. Wasn't the whole point for them to enjoy the game, to learn the game . . . to be on a team? Would not the mixing of the *talent* so that different combinations of kids were playing at the same time from game to game have been a more balanced plan? A more child-focused, age-appropriate plan?

And Francis remembers standing out in the cold, in the dead of winter, before daylight, watching little four-year-old babies get off the bus in zero-degree weather and thinking to himself, "This is madness! Surely we can have more flexibility with our bus schedules than this. These children don't need to be out on the road at this hour, and in this weather." He wishes he would have helped his district come up with some type of alternative since the transportation schedule was sometimes not aligned with what was best for kids.

Francis also remembers going to bat for elementary teachers to be paid a stipend for sponsoring student clubs after school, but being told that only the middle school and high school staff would be eligible for such perks. Reflecting now, he believes he backed off way too easily. He should have brought that simple suggestion up in meeting after meeting, year after year, as what resulted by not pressing the issue was less kids having the opportunity to get involved in after-school activities.

And what is sadder, in all of the instances just mentioned, the children from less privileged homes would have benefited the most if Francis had advocated more for the adults involved to work harder to meet the varying needs of all students. For many of the less fortunate, the parents don't know how to speak up and point out weak policies (or they are too intimidated to do so). If the principal or other school leaders don't stand in the gap, no one does.

But the one social injustice issue that stands out in his mind more than any other as Francis looks back over his career in school leadership is a complicated case that involved several students and the passing around of prescribed pills. These were middle schoolers. The incident blew up out of nowhere one afternoon, and Francis called the local police in to help with the investigation. Some prominent kids from the community had been right in the middle of the action, but the focus soon zeroed in on who had brought the meds to school, and who had started the whole thing. It seemed that one student, in special education and a young man of few words when trying to defend himself, was the instigator.

That Saturday morning, the local sheriff and Francis visited the boy's home. He lived in a humble dwelling with his family well out in the country, a long way from the school. Francis appeared before the board of education at its next monthly meeting, as members went into closed session to discuss what had been decided as punishment and to correct the situation. It was late when Francis got home that evening, almost midnight. But he was pleased, as the superintendent and the board agreed with his plan, and seemed to appreciate how thoroughly he had handled the incident without it becoming the talk of the community.

What was the plan? Francis placed the boy who had distributed the drugs in "in-school suspension" for several days, and he even had lunch during this stretch of time in an isolated, but visible, area at the end of the gym, away from his classmates. What did Francis do to the other kids? He warned them, and moved on. To be quite honest here, one of those parents in particular would have most likely sued the school district, and dragged everyone involved through months of grief if Francis had gone any other route with the lack of evidence he had on the other students.

As Francis remembers, the school never had another incident with drugs during his tenure at that school. He and the sheriff, working together, had sent a very strong message that such nonsense would not be tolerated, and severe consequences would be enforced. But as he looks back, he wonders: did he practice privileged thinking? Did he take the easy way out by conveniently using a scapegoat who certainly had no means to defend himself?

As time went on, what happened to the boys involved in this story? At least a couple of those who were merely warned went on to be involved in other incidents of disrespect and defiance, as they seemed to have some rebelliousness in them. And what happened to the special-education student who accepted the brunt of the punishment? He is no longer with us, apparently committing suicide as a young man a few years ago.

QUESTIONS FOR REFLECTION

1. Think of a time when your school seemed to take the convenient way out of a volatile situation due to a "privileged thinking" mindset.
2. Are there specific issues currently in your school or district that need to be addressed due to social injustices polluting the school culture?
3. Some argue that sports are specifically designed to separate out the best athletes—a survival-of-the-fittest mentality that is, to a degree, an underlying principle of capitalism and the American way of life. Others bitterly disagree, citing that recreational opportunities in the school setting do not have to always be about winning as the ultimate objective. Discuss.
4. Why are elementary teachers traditionally not given stipends for sponsoring after-school cocurricular and extracurricular activities?

SUGGESTIONS FOR FURTHER READING:

Middleton, K., and E. Pettit. (2007). *Who Cares?* Tucson, AZ: Wheatmark.
Sergiovanni, T. J. (2005). *Strengthening the Heartbeat.* San Francisco: Jossey-Bass.

Chapter 5

I Have a Name

She walked quietly to her next class, realizing that it was almost the end of the first semester. Yet, one of her teachers still didn't even know her name.

Today's typical school faculty finds itself in a precarious environment, often asked to work daily with hundreds of students in these large, mall-like structures we call schools. These massive daytime *cities*—sprawling campuses that impress the casual observer with their expanse of modern space and seemingly endless resources—can turn out to be (at least for some students and staff) very impersonal places. The key is in the detail, the very critical detail of the one-to-one *relationship*.

In the rush to somehow educate the masses in an industrial-age assembly line model (with far too little human resources afforded to meet such a task), the American schooling system has too often—at least in some schools and some classrooms—missed the whole point. The natural result of an authentic, heart-to-heart relationship between the mentor and the pupil is that both parties benefit as they learn and grow together. Oxford University goes so far as to require this one–to-one interaction in doctoral studies: one mentor to one pupil throughout the program, until the dissertation is defended. Can you imagine what participating in this model must be like? How rich! How life transforming!

Yet, such exception to the traditional paradigm of a "twenty to one" or "thirty to one" student-teacher ratio is rare. A former college student shares that he had been in one course that was four hundred to one! Wonder if he had even one meaningful discussion with the professor of that class?

Yes, granted, many schools, especially preschools and grade schools, are blessed to have instructional assistants, volunteers, and fellow teacher specialists who work with students individually and in smaller groups for much of the day. And perhaps this is why students very candidly share that their memories of elementary school reflect back on a happy time in their lives—a time of creativity, play, and an abundance of classroom experiences being a part of school—a school culture that was safe and warm, a family atmosphere.

But somewhere along the way, educators bought into the myth that older kids don't need the affection, the individual attention, the abundance of creativity and community built into their days at school. Oh yes, students are encouraged to be in community among their peers. But is every student also experiencing community with their mentors (their teachers)? Despite an alarming high-school dropout rate that across the board in this country is close to 30 percent for students in ninth through twelfth grades, the system still plugs along with the same outdated models. Those outside the field must look on in amazement and most likely can be heard whispering: "They just don't get it, do they?"

The bottom line is not a complex principle. In fact, it's the very basic of any successful venture that involves human beings working together. Life is about relationship. Family is about relationship. Adult work from day to day throughout one's career is about relationship. And school is about relationship. The one variable that has been too often overlooked in all of the searching for better answers in how American schools should be run is the timeless core value of the trusting, ethical, authentic mentor-pupil relationship.

In thinking back over one's life, and the many, many people who have had such a positive impact on that life, the non-negotiable that always rises to the surface is *relationship*. If people don't connect, and in some instances don't even know each other's names, they're certainly not on a short list of influencers who took time to care.

A former teacher shares a personal example from the first year he taught. Just home from college, he was hired as an elementary physical education teacher and coach of two sports. What fond memories he still has of earning the privilege to be called a *teacher!* The local school district had been operating without any PE specialists in the elementary grades, and thus he was handed seven schools and 2,200 students. Oh my! Was it a challenge? Yes. Was it fulfilling? Yes. Did the young educator learn every child's name? No. Was it feasible to even come close to creating a mentor-pupil bond with a majority of his students? No.

And today, when he runs into former students from those early years in his career, invariably, if he had learned their name and paid attention to them in class, they recognize him, and speak fondly of their memories of those days in elementary PE. But if he hadn't connected, not only would he still not know their name, but they now wouldn't remember his name either. He had invested much training, time, and sacrifice for their PE classes to be special and state of the art. But what they needed most, *all of them,* was for their PE teacher to know their name . . . especially those who were from under-privileged backgrounds and perhaps already starting to struggle in school. Elementary kids love PE class. What an opportunity this young teacher had to make connections by being a role model who cared!

We naively wonder why the "lost kids," the low achievers, the troublemak-ers, the dropouts, and those who form their anti-establishment gangs seem to turn on us as they get older. Perhaps, they have little choice. Perhaps, however unintentionally, we turn our backs on them somewhere along the way, and they realize the harsh reality that a teacher doesn't even know their name.

QUESTIONS FOR REFLECTION

1. What measures does your school take to ensure that *all* students have a variety of opportunities to connect with staff one-to-one and in small groups?
2. How are you addressing the dilemma of declining budgets and larger class sizes?
3. Does your staff professional development program routinely include the research on emotional intelligence, and how to build healthy relationships with students?
4. In a future faculty meeting, survey teachers and develop some data on the kids in your school who do not have at least one adult in the school setting who is mentoring them at this stage of their educational career.

SUGGESTIONS FOR FURTHER READING:

Kohn, A. (1999). *The Schools Our Children Deserve.* New York: Houghton Mifflin Company.
Maxwell, J. C. (2010). *Everyone Communicates—Few Connect.* Nashville: Thomas Nelson.

Chapter 6

Squeaky Wheels Get the Grease—But Some Don't Know How to Squeak

College-educated parents for the most part know how to navigate the system. They know who to go to, what to ask, and how to ask. They have taken speech and debate in college. They have learned to be persistent. They work in a world of words, and the words flow freely. Parents who are also teachers even more so know the questions to ask as advocates for their children. They know what to listen for to determine who are the best teachers and who would be the best teacher for their child. Parents who are teachers feel that it is their "right," a "perk" if you will, to request a particular teacher for their child.

Who will be the advocate for those who do not know how to squeak? Who do not know the questions to ask? Who are intimidated by the scholarly tongue of educators?

Is it just when some students get to be assigned to the teacher of their choice and others do not? Should it be a "perk" of being a parent to have the option of requesting a particular teacher for his or her child when others do not have that same opportunity?

Each spring some schools across the country allow parents to list their top three choices for teachers for their children for the following school year. Many a principal will say, "They *all* had the opportunity, but you would be surprised to see that very few parents, especially those of our high-risk, low-performing, and low socioeconomic status students, take advantage of this or even take the time to turn in the forms. They just don't seem to care."

Is it really *not caring?* Is it really the lack of *taking the time?* Do these parents know what makes a good teacher? Are they in the loop to discuss the pros and cons of educators in the schools their children attend? When school test score information becomes available to the public, are they knowledgeable enough to interpret that data?

Perhaps the real question to ask is, "Who among the faculty is someone parents would prefer that their child did *not* have as a teacher?" This is the tough question school administrators and leaders must lay on the table. *It is not fair for any child* to have a weaker teacher.

Educators should not assume that when parents do not come forward, it is because they do not care. Some just do not know how. Parents go to the principal's office when their children are late because the car broke down. They go to court for their child's absences when they have their child take care of a younger sibling or elderly grandparent while Mom goes off to work to put food on the table. Children get behind in school work when there is not one person with a high school degree at home to help them with it. Many times their previous experiences in schools have not been pleasant ones.

Ruby Payne's work in understanding children of poverty states that children from a low socioeconomic status background do not have the vocabulary that those with more privileged means have. These kids then become the parents of children who don't know the questions to ask or how to ask them.

QUESTIONS FOR REFLECTION

1. What can we do in our schools to help these parents and ultimately help these kids?
2. Are we creating injustices in our school when we allow people to select a teacher? What does this say about our faculty?
3. How do we—or *can we*—involve and educate parents of *all* socioeconomic backgrounds?

SUGGESTIONS FOR FURTHER READING:

Senge, P., Cambron-McCabe, N., Lucas, T., Smith, B., Dutton, J., and A. Kleiner. (2000). *Schools That Learn: A Fifth Discipline Fieldbook for Educators, Parents and Everyone Who Cares About Education.* New York: Doubleday.
Payne, R. (1996). *Framework for Understanding Poverty.* Highlands, TX: Aha Process Inc.

Chapter 7

Rigid Master Schedules

He learned how to play a guitar on the back porch of his uncle's house during the summer when he was ten years old. By fourteen, he was in a traveling band. He dropped out of school as soon as he could to make a living with his music. Besides, his high school didn't offer guitar lessons, anyway.

In taking a look inward to assess how schools can more effectively combat social injustice, one huge area that provides an array of possibilities is the master schedule. A school's total menu of student services is dependent on how mobile and versatile the master schedule is, and on how focused the district and staff is on providing a comprehensive offering of curricular, cocurricular, and extracurricular learning experiences for its students.

Consider the senior year of a high school girl, and how master schedule inflexibility cost her something she had worked hard for. She had been studying music since she was five years old, and had played drums in the high school band for years. She also loved basketball, and was very good at it. But when she asked to do both, her band director basically said, "Make up your mind—one or the other." She chose basketball, and went on to excel at playing the game for four years in college. But she never picked up her drum sticks again to share her skills in music that had taken years to perfect.

Another girl, while in middle school, was told she could not take both chorus and band, even though her mother tried to explain that she was passionate about both and would most likely study music in college. To no avail: the computerized master schedule won out, and the young student never did participate in middle school or high school band from that point on. She did indeed go on to major in music education in college, and has a master's degree in music as well. Her mom was right on target about what her daughter had a passion for, but the *system* seemed to not be as focused on her specific learning needs and interests.

Many students are raised in blessed homes. Their parents are huge advocates of education, and they provide a healthy environment for the child as a whole (at whatever stage of life), always standing in the gap for each of their children to make sure they develop in every area they have *any* interests in—academics, extracurricular activities, hobbies, community activities, church, etc. But what about the many kids who don't have such strong support from home? Perhaps both parents work just to make ends meet. Perhaps the parents are divorced. Perhaps one or both are disabled, or deceased, or suffering from an addiction of some kind. Perhaps they don't value education and the critical role parents should play in advocating for their children.

For these kids, who deserve the same opportunities to cultivate their talents and to chase their dreams as their classmates, the school philosophy in regard to *menu of student services* is critical. Does the master schedule rule the school? Or does relationship, community, and the equipping of students for a fulfilling life have the final say? Schools that are making the biggest difference, and carving out new opportunities for students every year, have a "can do" culture that chooses the latter philosophy.

How can educators know more about the many individual interests of students? Ask them! Exit interviews with students as they are finishing their last year at school provide wonderful insights into what they experienced that went well, and into what they needed but didn't experience. Parents will also provide invaluable feedback—if asked. In fact, sadly, many parents will confide that they realized later that the needs of their child (or children) were not met in the P–12 years, as they should have been. Would it have made a difference if they had been routinely asked to suggest ways to improve their child's school, and if those suggestions had been taken seriously? Yes, it would have made a *huge* difference!

Parents will wistfully share comments such as, "She was a gifted writer, but school seemed to kill her thirst for it as she got older." Or, "He loved cars, but there was not time for that in school." Or, "She has always loved drama, from the time she was a little girl. But they didn't offer that much at her high school, so she didn't even go to college. She's working at a dead-end job, and very unhappy." Or, "My son always wanted to be a conservation officer. I always wondered why there wasn't an outdoor club at his school, with so many of his friends loving to hunt and fish, and enjoy the outdoors. He didn't do well on the state exam that would have qualified him to work at a state park, so he's bagging groceries and hoping to get on at the local sports gear shop."

And the examples could go on and on of former students who would agree that their P–12 days somehow missed the mark. A former school principal who assumed his son would be given a scholarship to college since his ACT score was over 30, was shocked when his son's senior year arrived, but there had not been much done on his behalf. It seemed he wore a trench coat, and ran with the unconventional crowd, so apparently the school subconsciously wrote him off!

Perhaps this kid didn't listen in sessions with juniors and seniors that went over how to apply for college scholarships. Perhaps he didn't go into the counselor's office with a clean haircut and a firm handshake, and ask, "Will you help me?" But should he have had to "play the game" to have been taken seriously with an ACT of 30? Good grief! The system failed him and his family, plain and simple.

And then there's the similar case of a student who had a very high ACT score, but kept putting off filling out his college application. Finally, his principal called the school this boy desired to go to, and they revealed that he had missed the deadline. Upon further query, the principal found out that the family was scared to let the boy go away to school, and that most likely, they did not know *how* to fill out the endless maze of paperwork for entrance into college. She became relentless in getting this uniquely gifted and talented kid into college. She helped him get enrolled in the local community college that fall, and within a year, he was on his way to the school he had longed to go to originally.

What made the difference? Someone took the time to care. Someone essentially said, "You are not going to mess up your life on my watch. You *are* going to college. And I will help you make that happen. So, pull up a chair. We've got some paperwork to fill out—right now." This boy was not from a privileged home. How many more like him are out there? How many more will fall through the cracks before educators admit that a part of the system is terribly broken?

When a high percentage of a graduating class of seniors is not in some type of post-secondary training and doing well the following fall semester, it is quite obvious that something is out of balance. Something in the web of support has gone awry. After all, counting early childhood classes, many kids have been in school for 14 years when they walk across the stage on their graduation night (*if* they've survived the system long enough to walk across the stage).

QUESTIONS FOR REFLECTION

1. What is your school's approach to the philosophy of *every* student being on an individualized learning plan?
2. How does your school go about adjusting its menu of services based on student surveys and expressed needs (as well as needs that assessment data

reveals)? If you are at a high school, how does your school mentor and coach juniors and seniors through the maze of post-secondary applications and scholarship assistance? Are *all* juniors and seniors afforded the same depth of support?

3. How many student clubs does your school offer? Do volunteers from the community have the opportunity to assist with your cocurricular and extracurricular programs?

4. What is your school's process for proactively assisting students with the development of specific interests and talents? Are students allowed to audit certain portions of classes? Would a student who has a passion for gymnastics or arts and crafts or farming, for example, have an opportunity to pursue any of these interests further at your school?

SUGGESTIONS FOR FURTHER READING:

Gladwell, M. (2008). *Outliers—The Story of Success.* New York: Little, Brown, and Company.

Tushman, M. L., and C. A. O'Reilly III. (2002). *Winning through Innovation.* Boston: Harvard Business School Press.

Chapter 8

Skateboarders

Unfit for Social Justice

Don't those skateboarders immediately turn you off? Literally! Aren't they all alike, with their baggy pants and long hair, and behaving in an inconsiderate and defiant way? Do they ever stay on their own property (as if their families had any)? Like drug addicts or gang members, they will likely be dead or in jail by the time they reach twenty-one years of age, won't they? Forget social justice for them! Right?

Wrong! Stereotyping is never good, regardless of whom it is directed at! Skateboarders are people too, and it is privileged thinking and social injustice that not only perpetuate the myth about this primary (and coveted) pastime of many of our students but also cast them to subordinate roles in schools and prevent their academic and social progress. Too often they are not only ignored, but abhorred!

This topic of privileged thinking and social injustice is quite complex, and there is no simple solution to complex problems. It is so pervasive in American communities that it will invariably be reflected in our schools. Did administrators not learn early on in their leadership training that schools are a reflection of the communities they serve, that whatever you find in the community, including drugs and crime, will ultimately surface in the schools?

Privileged thinking and social injustice regarding skateboarders was evident at a large high school (1,500 students) in the late 1990s and early 2000s. Perhaps this came about because most of the students involved were from low SES homes, performed poorly academically, were for the most part not supervised by their parents, were not involved in extracurricular activities, and often had discipline problems.

Tom Young (a name used to protect the anonymity of the actual student involved) was from a single-parent home, had four siblings, would not do his academic work, and was often referred to the office for disciplinary reasons. One day after school the principal saw him come on campus riding his skateboard and noticed that almost immediately he was escorted off school property by a staff member who at the same time appeared to be giving Tom a good lecture (tongue-lashing!). The next day when the principal saw Tom between classes—and at a time when he was not in trouble—he said, "Tom, I'd like to talk with you about how we could promote skateboarding at our school. When would be a good time for you to come to my office for a discussion?"

Tom responded that he would talk with the principal and that he could pick the time. Since Tom lived near the school, it was suggested that the meeting take place that day. Knowing that he was pretty much on his own, the principal asked if he needed to go home first, get permission from his mom, and then come back to talk. He replied, "Naw, she won't care!"

That afternoon Tom and the principal talked and it led to:

- Skateboarders being allowed to bring (not ride) their skateboards with them each school day with the understanding that they would leave them at the front office.
- Skateboarders being allowed to pick up their boards after school and skate in a designated area in the front—not back—of the building after the buses and student drivers had left.
- Skateboarders being allowed to skate during the school day in front of their peers during "student appreciation" activities that were held a couple times per year.
- Three skateboarders, another staff member, and the principal traveling during the school day to Lexington (Kentucky's second-largest city) to visit a skate park to gather ideas to present to the local mayor—with the hopes that a skate park could be built there.
- Tom, another skateboarder, and the principal meeting with both the mayor and county judge executive to get pledges of thousands of dollars to begin a skate park on a site suggested by the mayor and owned by the city.

These initiatives began during the spring of 2002. As a result, skateboarders became better citizens of the school; the scowl left many of their faces; Tom became the leader of the Skateboarders Club; the principal was hired to be superintendent of a nearby school district; and the mayor promised to keep alive the intent to build a skateboard park. However, the park was never built and the principal never followed up on how skateboarding and boarders fared after he left the school in 2002.

This story is shared because the principal remembered what a shock it was for the privileged thinkers—staff, students, and parents—when they learned that he was not only conversing with, but allowing, instead of condemning, skateboarding. Why, he was even allowing students to carry their boards right into the main office, secure them after school, and skate in front of visitors and many others who often had business to conduct at the school long after the regular school day was over! And what if they got hurt, or hurt someone else? Surely the school district's insurance would not cover such, would it?

Did they think that the principal was not prudent or wise enough to cover the bases on the insurance and liability issues before setting up this privilege for the skateboarders? Could skateboarding be any more dangerous than football? Were they surprised the principal would take the time to discuss skateboarding with the insurance company and superintendent, or the time to take some of them to Lexington to gain information that would be helpful in building a skate park in their county? Was that not quite audacious of the principal, and should he not be spending that time working on improving academic achievement for kids who really cared about their learning and not on a bunch of renegades?

Though these were some of the natural reactions/responses of the privileged thinkers at the school, they later seemed amazed at how well the skateboarders handled the responsibilities and privileges they had been granted. They never skated on the school grounds in the mornings. They always carried their boards to school and were gentlemanly in their behavior and attitude as they deposited them in the front office each morning and secured them at the end of the school day. They would pick up their boards if they were near individuals who were entering or leaving the building during their afternoon skating episodes.

Through no choice of their own, students, staff, and parents got closer to skateboarders during the spring of 2002 than most of them ever had in their entire lives. Previously, their privileged and stereotypical thinking persuaded them to stay as far from these students as possible. Yet when skateboarders were rendered social justice, when their activity was legitimized, it was not long before bewilderment and anger on the part of the masses became amusement and acceptance. Skateboarders became transparent, not threatening. At student appreciation day activities they were at times the center of attention, watched and applauded as they performed in the designated area. Even the superintendent, associate superintendent, and director of instruction came from the central office and watched these students.

The principal later had two regrets relating to this experience with skateboarders at this high school. One, though he was enormously busy at the end of the 2001–2002 school year assuming the superintendent's position of a large Kentucky school district, he felt he should have found the time to work with the principal who succeeded him and the skateboarders to keep the skateboard park initiative alive with the city mayor and county judge executive. And two, he should have given the names of the dozen or so students involved to the head of the school's guidance department and had him specifically follow their grades, discipline records, and graduation rate. That is what he recommends for those future leaders who initiate examples of social justice for the non-privileged thinkers in their schools.

QUESTIONS FOR REFLECTION

1. Are we doing another kind of injustice to students when we endorse activities such as skateboarding, when we should be focusing on their academic achievement, and their involvement in activities such as sports that are more widely accepted by the masses, and that are not so dangerous? Support your answer.
2. Would Tom Young ever have thought that he would have the opportunity to start and lead a skateboarders club at his high school? Why or why not?
3. Will students like Tom, who are not privileged thinkers and who suffer social injustice, ever have the courage to speak for themselves and be courageous enough—or even have the articulation skills—to ask for the kind of consideration given him and his friends? Why or why not?
4. Can a principal provide the time and opportunities to such a group as skateboarders, as described in this case, without compromising opportunities for the remainder of the student body? Support your answer.
5. Tom and his friends were members of the freshman and sophomore classes during the 2001–2002 school year. If the principal had asked the head counselor to follow up on their academic, behavioral, and graduation progress, speculate on what the results may have been in 2004, the year they were to graduate, assuming that the successor kept the program intact.

SUGGESTIONS FOR FURTHER READING:

Marshall, C., and M. Olivia. (2010). _Leadership for Social Justice; Making Revolutions in Education._ Boston: Allyn & Bacon.
Fleming, N. L. (1980). _A Study of the Relationship between Student Perception of the Organizational Climate of the Schools and Student Achievement._ Utah State University: Dissertation Abstracts International, Vol. 41/10-A, 1980.

Chapter 9

Throw Them a Life-Preserver, Not an Anchor

Life preservers are thrown to people when they are going under. The purpose they serve is to keep one afloat until help arrives. Too often educators think they are throwing students floatation devices, assuming they are helping, when in fact they are hurting. They might as well throw them an anchor.

Many times, schools proudly promote all of the wonderful programs they have to offer students. They boast of after-school and before-school tutoring. They host evening parent sessions on how to help kids at home with school work. They develop schedules where parents can call in and make an appointment to meet with their child's team of teachers. And then they sadly boast of how the students taking advantage of such programs are the students who are working hard to not get a C in a class, and the parents that come are not the ones they really hoped would show.

It is here that educators often become critical in analyzing the problem. They say these kids and parents are lazy. They say these parents do not value education. They remark, even make fun of, how this population of students and parents will come to a dance or a ball game before they will show for a teacher conference.

It is privileged thinking that prevents the trained professionals from looking deeper at the real issues here. To illustrate, Sue came from a rural background, born and raised in the country, the youngest of five siblings. Her parents graduated from high school but neither, at the time, attended college. They were from average means. Sue's family never had a great deal, but they never wanted for much. They had food, they had shelter, and they had each other. Vacation to them meant a camping trip or a day at a ball field somewhere. Sue had never noticed what her family did *not* have and *never really realized how much they did have* . . . until she became a school administrator.

If Sue would have needed to stay after school for some extra tutoring with a teacher, her parents would have made arrangements to have her stay. If the teachers needed to talk with her parents, they were just a phone call away. Sue's mother was a stay-at-home mom and pretty much at the house all day, doing what moms did then—cleaning, canning, gardening, cooking, making jellies, that sort of thing. Sue thought that was what everyone's mom did!

Sue's father came home every evening without fail around 5:30 after work. He quickly did some chores, and the family all sat down to dinner in a timely manner at 6:00. After dinner, they all had their assigned chores for cleaning up, then it was time to hit the books, do the homework, take a bath, and then off to bed.

When Sue became a principal she suddenly realized that *not all* kids were raised like her. She was frustrated when the students who needed the most help never took advantage of the assistance that was offered. She wondered and also made judgments such as, "What kind of parents are these who do not get their kids the help they need? And the help is free at that!"

Then Sue had an epiphany: these parents were just like hers. They loved their kids, these parents cared deeply about their children, but they did not have the means of getting them to and from the morning or after-school interventions the school offered. As a school principal, Sue realized you can offer wonderful programs all you want. Your list can be endless. But of what value are they if they are helpful only to the privileged families? Sue thought she had the heart to feel what these families feel and programs to help. Sue never thought of herself as privileged, until she realized what many of her students went home to.

At Sue's school, her staff offered programs, but they did not offer transportation. The parents wanted their kids to come, and the kids wanted the help. But who was to provide transportation? Only those who had the extra car or a stay-at-home mom took advantage.

But what about the dances and ball games these kids seem to get to, you say? Yes, they do seem to attend these more. But if you have ever studied children of poverty, they live in a world that may not see tomorrow. So to come to a joyous event perhaps is more important, as they cannot see beyond the moment in the oftentimes chaotic world they live in.

So the next time you create a program that you believe is giving your students a lifeline, check and see if it is not an anchor you are throwing them. If these students are not coming, analyze what the anchor is that is keeping them from attending.

QUESTIONS FOR REFLECTION

1. What intervention programs does your school have in place? *Who* is not showing and *why? What* is the anchor? How can your staff level the playing field?
2. When it comes to providing tutoring or immediate interventions, perhaps the staff needs to look at the school schedule and what is offered between 8:30 and 3:30, within the school day. It is here *all students* are a captive audience. To effectively be a lifeline of support, what is your school offering during the school day time frame?
3. What suggestions do you have for your school's master schedule so it is not such a barrier to students who need more intervention support?

SUGGESTIONS FOR FURTHER READING:

Blankstein, A. (2004). *Failure Is Not an Option: Six Principles That Guide Student Achievement in High Performing Schools.* Thousand Oaks, CA: Corwin Press and the Hope Foundation.

Gurian, M. (2001). *Boys and Girls Learn Differently: A Guide for Teachers and Parents.* San Francisco: Jossey-Bass.

Chapter 10

No Band for the Kid
from Lucky Stop

Many of us have our own rags to riches story, though poverty and wealth are more often than not in the eye of the beholder. Following is a true story of how privileged thinking and social injustice may have kept a poor fifth-grade student from being in the band but not from becoming superintendent of that school district. Is that a paradox, or what?

Born in 1946 in southeastern Kentucky (Perry County), the twelfth of fourteen children to a father (coal miner) with a third-grade education and a stay-at-home mother who finished eighth grade, Jon was later to realize that the culture of that section of the Appalachian Mountains would have an everlasting impact on his life, both personally and professionally. He has always been exceedingly proud of his eastern Kentucky heritage!

What actually happened to the coal industry after World War II that caused his father to pick up roots with his wife and nine children (those still at home) and move to Pleasant Run in rural Morgan County was never clear to Jon. All he knew was that in the fall of 1950, the family ended up there with the task of helping his maternal grandfather run a sawmill. And in July of 1951, he began his public-education experience in a one-room school, grades one through eight, with one other student and himself comprising the entire first grade.

Before that first-grade year was over, in February 1952, his family had moved further west to Camargo, a small town five miles south of Mt. Sterling, in Montgomery County, where the owners of the house the family rented had promised his dad and older brothers a job on the farm. Those jobs never materialized, but his dad was lucky enough to get a job as a custodian because the brother of the owner of the house the family was renting was on the school board, and school board members did the hiring in those days—and the property owners wanted their monthly rent! For the next ten years or so, Jon's dad was a custodian (called a janitor in those days) at various schools in the county, and the children would help him. There was not a room in the school system that Jon did not sweep at one time or another!

Three years later, by the time he entered third grade at Camargo School, the family had moved ten miles southeast of Mt. Sterling to a little wide spot in the road called Lucky Stop! An older gentleman who lived there lent Jon's dad $500 to buy a strip of land along the top of a cliff (literally).

A family in Camargo had decided to tear down an old, two-story wooden home and replace it with a brick one. Jon's family was told that if they would tear the old house down, they could have the lumber. By this time the ages of the four boys at home ranged from seven to sixteen, and an older brother had returned from the army. They carefully tore the house down, saved the lumber—and even the metal (sheets of tin) from the roof and the nails—hauled the materials to Lucky Stop, straightened the nails, and built an A-frame type of house with a porch on each end—the place where Jon lived until he got married. His parents lived there until their deaths in the mid 1990s.

After having lived in Lucky Stop for two years, Jon entered fifth grade and was enormously excited one day at school when the announcement was made that a new band director had been hired to serve multiple schools in the county school district, and all students interested in joining the band were to report to the gymnasium for a meeting. Though he had already learned to love basketball and had played the game on outside goals that his dad had in some way always managed to provide the boys (in those days there were no basketball programs for girls), nothing had ever piqued his interest and excitement as much as that announcement. Jon thought to be able to play in the band would be the best thing to ever happen to him!

The meeting with the new band director went wonderfully well. He was very likable and said that all the students would need in order to get their instruments and be in the band was a $10-per-month instrument rental fee. Jon knew money was tight, but he could not restrain his excitement and enthusiasm, even optimism, as the school day ended and he traveled to the janitor's room to see his dad, share his excitement, and get a commitment for the $10 per month. His dad was very loving and understanding, but being the sole breadwinner with a salary of $150 per month (and the family was never on free lunch, nor did they ever receive any government assistance such as food stamps or any other benefit), he had to say no to Jon's request. Jon was crushed, but he knew to never again say anything about joining the band—and he didn't!

Because his dad was always able to talk the local basketball coaches out of an old basketball from time to time, and would allow Jon and his siblings to play basketball in the gymnasium when their janitorial tasks were done, Jon became a pretty good basketball player and found that all he had to provide was tennis shoes in order to play on the teams. And once you made varsity (A-team in that day), even your tennis shoes were provided. That was something he could afford, and in the long term, sports (he also played baseball and ran cross-country) were good for him and became his ticket to college.

With zero financial support from his parents, Jon was able to get a BA, an MA, a Rank I, and an EdD, becoming a teacher, coach, principal and superintendent in the very school system he had helped his dad sweep the rooms. This was the same school system that had been unable to provide social justice to a fifth grader whose career in band actually began and ended on the same day—when he was asked to provide money beyond his family's ability if he wanted to stay in the band.

Some would say that privileged thinking on the part of the band director and the school administration, and the subsequent social injustice of disallowing Jon's involvement in the band, proved to be a blessing for him as it forced him to focus on sports, an arena in which there has been very little, if any, privileged thinking and social injustice. Coaches are notorious for their focus on winning and do not seem to care about race, color, religion, intelligence level, or socioeconomic status as long as one can put points on the board and/or otherwise help them to win.

Jon thinks differently, because from experience he believes there are innumerable students who are not athletically inclined but for whom music works out wonderfully. Stifling their interest and enthusiasm for music at an early age could be a negative, life-changing experience. Though Jon lettered in three sports in high school and college, he did not make it to the professional level.

Would Jon have achieved beyond the college level in music had he been given a chance to enter the band program at the age of ten, and subsequently devoted the time to music that he did to sports? What if athletics had not, for one reason or another, worked out for him? Would the absence of involvement in music resulted in his dropping out of school or not attending college? With this in mind, when he became a principal and superintendent, he gave enormous moral and financial support to band and orchestra programs and made it clear that no student should be turned away because of the lack of an instrument.

Privileged thinking and social injustice prohibited the kid from Lucky Stop from being in the band, but his eastern Kentucky heritage and indomitable spirit allowed him to lead the entire school system!

QUESTIONS FOR REFLECTION

1. Explain why the cost of any academic or extracurricular program offered by the school should, or should not, prohibit student participation.

2. If the school offers a program that a student cannot afford, is the administration guilty of privileged thinking? Why or why not?
3. Couldn't students and their parents find the money if they are really interested and committed to the class or activity, and render such scenarios as
   the one explained in this chapter a choice on the part of the family, instead
   of a social injustice on the part of the school? Explain.
4. If you are or have been a principal, give examples of how you ensured
   that money did not prevent any student from participating in classes and
   activities offered by the school. If you have never been a principal, picture
   yourself in that role and expound on how you think you would handle this
   dilemma.

SUGGESTIONS FOR FURTHER READING:

Green, R. L. (2010). *The Four Dimensions of Principal Leadership.* Boston: Allyn
   & Bacon.
Goodlad, J. I. (1979). *What Schools Are For.* Bloomington, IN: Phi Delta Kappan
   Educational Foundation.

Chapter 11

No Hamburgers or Salads for the Free Lunch Kids

Highly intelligent, well-meaning, caring staff members from the super-intendent on down to the cafeteria manager can be guilty, surely uncon-sciously, of allowing privileged thinking to trump social justice. Can you imagine a scenario at a large high school in which the students on free lunch were clearly treated differently from those who paid? And the adults in the environment did not seem to "get it."

Persuading a high percentage of high school students to eat in the cafeteria has always been an extraordinarily difficult task for principals and staff. A very popular strategy to deal with this, initiated in the early 1980s in many Kentucky schools, was to add a variety of choices. When during the summer of 1986 a new principal, Ralph Holmes, arrived at a large high school (1,600 students) in central Kentucky, he felt quite pleased, knowing that it was one of the state's largest schools; moreover, it was located in what was, and remains, one of Kentucky's nicest and most progressive small towns (population about 8,000 at the time). On the first day that lunch was served, as the 1986–1987 school year began, a school culture issue literally startled the new principal.

Perhaps he should not have been so surprised. Soon after arriving on the scene in early July, the two assistant principals accompanied him on a tour of the building, a very large facility first occupied in 1964. Though summer cleaning was in progress, a couple of issues jumped out at him: (1) excessive writing on the student desks and (2) an absence of privacy stalls (that's right, just stand alone commodes!), soap, mirrors, and hand towels (even tissue paper) in all boys' restrooms!

The principal asked, "What happened to the stalls?" An assistant answered, "The students kept tearing them down so we quit putting them up!" This was

41

followed by a rhetorical question, "Why no mirrors, soap, hand driers or towels, and tissue paper?" The answer was, "The students won't take care of them. They tear them down, and as quickly as we provide rolls of toilet paper, they throw them into the commodes, so we quit playing that game. And by the way, this is where the boys smoke, and many of our fights occur in the restrooms!"

Upon being hired for this principal's position, Ralph knew some aspects of the school were out of control, but he did not know it was this bad! Before getting back to what he discovered that first day about the lunch program, let it be noted that between July 4 and mid-August of that year, Principal Holmes had stalls (walls) constructed around the commodes in the boys' restrooms, equipped them with tissue paper, and replaced the mirrors, soap dispensers, and hand driers. Also, he had the custodial staff take the doors off all boys' and girls' restrooms (though the building was twenty-two years old, there were barriers that prevented looking into the restrooms once the doors opened). Amazingly, this was the talk of the community even before school started: "Did you hear what that new principal did? Says he is going to clean up that school. Why, he even took all the doors off the restrooms!"

On the first day of class at this high school in August 1986, the new principal continued a practice that he had begun while working as the principal at another high school: he had the entire student body and staff meet in the gymnasium for a welcome and awareness assembly, which included mention of rules, regulations, and expectations. And what a surprise! Though his two assistant principals had warned him that they had long before stopped having assembly programs due to atrocious student behavior, he never expected what he found. The students were wild and there was a complete absence of assembly etiquette! Yet, he did the best he could to talk over them and finish the assembly.

The next big surprise came during the lunch hour (actually, about a two-hour period, from 10:30–12:30), at the cafeteria, where Ralph found the school was providing three lines (choices): the regular line, consisting of a basic meal heavily reliant on government-provided commodities; the hamburger line; and the salad line. There was in place a rule that no one seemed to question: that students on free lunch had to go through the regular line. They could *not* have a salad or hamburger!

Ralph soon learned that an unrecognized stigma was attached to the regular line. It was for the poor kids only. Those who could pay for their lunch chose either the hamburger or salad lines. Participation in the regular line was enormously low, defeated the concept of choice, and explained why many students eligible for free lunch never applied, or did not participate, though approved.

To the surprise of students and staff (from the building level to the director of food services at the central office), Principal Holmes immediately announced that *all* lines were open to *all* students, and that set in motion a litany of strategies to change the culture of the school and to make it a place for *all* students. Without belaboring the point, inserted below is the speech given at the 1990 graduation ceremony by the senior class vice president. By this time, Ralph had completed four years as principal of this school, and the seniors knew that he had been hired as the new superintendent of a nearby school district and that he would be taking that position in a few days.

Here are the student's exact words, with the exception that the principal's name has been changed to protect his anonymity:

"There is a man among us tonight who has shown this school and this community what leadership abilities can do. Four years ago Dr. Ralph Holmes entered this school along with the class of 1990, and on that day in August of 1986 there began a series of changes that will mark this school forever. He told us if we break the mirrors, or tear down the toilet paper, he would only replace it with new. This whole attitude struck us as strange, but everyone enjoyed the respect he gave us and few things were damaged thereafter.

"He said, "Go ahead, write on the bathroom walls, we'll only repaint them!" Well, we wrote on the walls, and he kept his promise. He repainted them— brown, dark brown!!! With our best interest in mind, he took away our smoking areas. Although we couldn't caress or hold hands in the halls, we found an open-door policy to his office to talk about our concerns. The minor things which he took away—hats, sunglasses, and clothing with beer logos—were only incidental to the majority. He did all this with the reminder that it was all in the best interest of our education.

"It is easy to tell the effect Dr. Holmes has had upon this school. Under him our academics and athletics have flourished. He has made our school a place to be proud of, and he taught us all how to stand tall. That first day four years ago he stood in front of a student body who had no respect for him and we all yelled and screamed, paying no mind to his request for our attention. Now, four years later, he's the only man I know who can stand in front of 1,500 wild screaming teenagers and without saying a word, everyone stops talking, stops screaming, and they all turn their heads toward him waiting to hear what he's going to say. Because when Doc Holmes talks, everybody listens!

"We as a senior class bid you farewell, Dr. Holmes, and we hope your endeavors will prove to be as successful as they have been here. Dr. Holmes, please come forward. Please accept this gift as a small token of appreciation from the class of 1990, for making our four years here a memorable experience."

Shared now is one more component of the work at this school. When Principal Holmes mentioned the attention they were going to give to a poem he had written, some called him a "child of the 60s." He admitted the truthfulness of that statement but reminded them that even though he had graduated from high school and college during that decade, he did keep his head on straight during the time, did not do drugs, and had done a tour of duty in Vietnam

after having been drafted in 1969. It was during his second year as principal
at this school (Grand Roberts Central, also known as GRC) that he promised
an ALE81 (a popular soft drink) to any student who would submit a written
response—agreeing or disagreeing—with the poem below.

About 80 percent of the students actually submitted a written response
to their homeroom teachers, who then gave them to Dr. Holmes. Of those
submitted, over 90 percent were positive. Here is the poem:

SPL—GRC, by Ralph Holmes

Sunshine—
   that great light respected by all thinking people
     dispeller of darkness
       symbolic of happiness
         illustrative of knowledge, true and pure,
          abolishing ignorance
          and enhancing relationships.

Peace—
   that state of being sought by all thinking people
    peace within
      peace without
        needed by all
          opposite of war
            or any other idea
               antagonistic to man.

Love—
   that characteristic appreciated by all thinking people
    which all need
      to receive
        and to give,
          the soother of the negatives in life.

Grand Roberts Central—
   an institution in the process of
     Becoming.
       This school runs on
        sunshine,
          peace
            and
              love!

Tiresomely trite?
> *No!*

Idealistically realistic?
> *Yes!*

Note: While reading and reflecting on the above poem, the principal asked students if they would like for it to become the school's motto. Most applauded the positive changes in the school's climate but thought the slogan was "a little soft." The school continued to practice the poem's concepts, but it did not make it its slogan.

QUESTIONS FOR REFLECTION

1. Analyze the boys' restroom scenario and the lunch room practices found at this high school in 1986 for any evidence of privileged thinking and social injustice.
2. Teachers and administrators are characteristically caring and egalitarian. Evaluate why the school's staff and central office support people (including the superintendent) would allow such disciplinary problems and student inequities to emerge.
3. Typically, it is a given that from 80 to 100 percent of elementary students who qualify for free and reduced meals will apply, be approved, and participate on a regular basis, while about half of high school students will apply and less will participate. Is this the case in the schools you are familiar with, and if so, what has been done to get more high school students to apply and participate?
4. In most American Schools, we do not ask students to pay directly for such things as their books (particularly in K–8), bus transportation, teachers, buildings, and lockers. Why do we ask them to pay for their breakfast and lunch at school? Speculate on the impact on student achievement if we daily provided *all* students with free lunch and breakfast.

SUGGESTIONS FOR FURTHER READING:

Garlow, J. (2002). *The 21 Irrefutable Laws of Leadership; Tested by Time.* Nashville: Thomas Nelson Publishers.
Hartley, M., and W. K. Hoy. (1972). Openness of School Climate and Alienation of High School Students. *Journal of Educational Research*, 23 (1972), 17–24.

Chapter 12

One Child Left Behind

Everyone has different ways in which they learn—even different learning styles for learning different content.
 Why then do teachers not teach to the various learning styles of their students? When teaching something one way—often the one way that feels most comfortable—an educator is doing a social injustice to students at all levels. By teaching to one learning style, there will be many students left back—not just "one child left behind"—as a result of our educational negligence.

Yes, it does take time. It takes work. It takes resources and support. But ask yourself, "Where do I choose to spend my time, my work, my resources?"

To illustrate, a middle school principal had a teacher come to the office one day complaining that it took her over an hour to write up the stack of discipline referrals from her hectic day at school. She complained that the students just would not sit still and that they were incorrigible. The students were tuned up, tuned out, or turned off.

What would the outcome have been had this teacher given that one hour of her life before that day began to analyze her lesson plan and intentionally differentiate the day's activities to joyfully engage students, addressing the various learning styles? For sure, the day would have been much more pleasant and productive for everyone.

A student shared with the school counselor how she experienced injustice on a personal level in a pivotal year of her schooling, grade seven. New Math had come to town, and algebraic concepts were a part of this new curriculum. Due to some prior assessment scores, it was determined that Laura would be "tracked into the high section" for high-performing seventh graders. Once tracked, these students stayed with one another and moved throughout the day together in the same honors-level classes. That meant Laura was tracked in the high math class.

Laura's teacher, Mrs. Long, was a kind person, but you either learned it the way she taught it or you did not. Laura suddenly began to get Cs and Ds. Getting anything below a B was *not* acceptable in her home. Big Jim (her dad) was not happy with her declining math grades. Pressure from home and the added pressure from her cheerleading coach led to great anxiety. (An additional sidebar injustice to note: football players could maintain a D average and play, but cheerleaders had to maintain a B average to remain on the squad.) Was this just?

Laura was fortunate to have a sister, two years older, who loved math and did well in it. Laura's mom directed her sister to help Laura after dinner with math homework. Within an hour both girls were crying. The older sister was frustrated as to why Laura could not comprehend the material. Laura was crying because in health class she had just studied cancer and brain tumors, and she was now certain that she had one and this was what was preventing her from learning this math! She thought, "I am an A/B student starting to fail. I must have a brain tumor!" Then, an older sibling came to the table to lend assistance. He, too, became impatient with Laura, frustrated as to why she could not learn the math concepts. By now, Laura knew that she had only days to live!

Laura somehow survived the moment. But it has forever left an imprint on her view of math and . . . Mrs. Long.

As an adult, thinking back, Laura now knows why she did not "get it" with the help of her siblings. *They* all had Mrs. Long as a teacher years earlier. They were just giving Laura more of the same: the way Mrs. Long taught it years earlier to them. They learned how to do it through her teaching style. Laura did not.

Flash forward over twenty years from that moment, and one day, as an administrator, Laura was observing a collaborative math class. The regular education teacher covered the math concept that Laura remembered struggling with back in grade seven. The special education teacher then stood up and said, "Let me show you what Ms. Smith just did through these manipulatives." Suddenly, the understanding that seemed to have eluded Laura over twenty years earlier came to her instantly through the hands-on, concrete examples of the problems.

Does this seem like a minor injustice? It is a huge injustice that literally changes lives. Think about all of the students of poverty that do not have the supportive families behind them, who cannot afford extra tutoring, who have no one who can teach them the content in a manner in which they can learn it. Think of children who do not have people in their family with a high school or a college education to help them when they get home.

Think about the kids who play on a team or who are on the cheerleading squad and who, when they fail to learn, are sidelined and ineligible—or even worse, removed from the one thing that keeps them connected to school. Do we lose them, all because teachers such as Mrs. Long do not differentiate instruction in order to help *all* kids to be successful in the classroom?

The next time you get ready to prepare a lesson, remember how each student you come in contact with is unique. All of these students have the capability to learn if their mentors are capable of teaching in more than one way. Far too many students are failing *not* because they cannot learn, but because they are not being taught *so* they can learn. Each child is special, and educators should work diligently to not even have "one child left behind."

I Am Special . . . I Am Me, by Carol Christian

Sometimes adults don't listen . . . try to understand or see . . .
That I'm NOT like all the others . . .
I am special . . . I am me . . .

Some teachers tell me what to do . . .
What to think and say . . .
Because they think they're smarter . . .
I must do it all their *way.*

They think that learning's simple . . .
And one way *is all they teach.*
They don't let me be creative . . .
Try to think, explore or reach . . .

Some kids are better readers
Some good with numbers/math . . .
Some are followers . . . some are leaders . . .
Some take a different path.

Engage me in the learning . . .
Make it meaningful and real
Show me that you value HOW . . .
I learn best . . . and think . . . and feel.

Let me write it, read it, lead it
Let me move, reflect and draw . . .
I'll look back upon your teaching
In such wonderment and awe . . .

Let me feel it, see it, hear it.
In groups—alone—in pairs
To teach me you must know me first
It helps when someone cares.

It's not *that* I can't—*I'm different*
It's just my learning style
Some content I learn faster,
In others . . . it takes awhile.

Engage me, wake me, lead me . . .
Inspire my will to learn . . .
Ignite the spirit in me
My utmost respect . . . you then will earn.

And if you do—I'll "thank you"
In working hard to make me see . . .
That in teaching so many different ways . . .
I became the best that I can be . . .

QUESTIONS FOR REFLECTION

1. What is your favored learning style? Does this style remain constant, or have you found it varies according to the situation?
2. Describe a time when you had an insight and taught something a different way, and you were surprised how many more students were able to grasp the material. How did the students respond?
3. Far too many high school teachers do not differentiate instruction. What do you think the real issue is here? Time? Know-how? Fear of failure? Fear of the unfamiliar? Is it the lack of knowledge in being able to teach something more than one way? When you are in one of these situations, do you turn to your colleagues for ideas?

SUGGESTIONS FOR FURTHER READING:

Silver, H., R. Strong, and M. Perini. (2000). *So Each May Learn—Integrating Learning Styles and Multiple Intelligences.* Alexandria, VA: Association for Supervision and Curriculum Development.

Marzanno, R. (2002). *What Works in Schools—Translating Research into Action.* Alexandria, VA: Association for Supervision and Curriculum Development.

Tomlinson, C. (2001). *How to Differentiate Instruction in Mixed Ability Classrooms.* Alexandria, VA: Association for Supervision and Curriculum Development.

Chapter 13

The School Within the Lines

*A child who is asked to conform to the extent that he or she doesn't feel
like a unique individual anymore, is a child that has been victimized by
the "system"—a system that is drawn toward cookie-cutter models, and
toward linear protocol that embraces mediocrity if it keeps the masses in
their assigned roles.*

Some argue that for every student that the system of schooling benefits (by
opening doors to a bright and exciting future), there is another that somehow
did not learn how to "play the game." Thus, one can only hope that the sur-
vivors of the bureaucratic nature of *school* land on their feet and do well. A
somewhat bizarre game of chance, isn't it? It sorts out winners and losers
not by how well the safety net is designed, but by how well the players learn
to navigate, literally, from the time they start school. For those from the
homes of comfort and affluence, the odds are much better. But even then, the
adults who create and manipulate the system can be so lost in the day-to-day
assumptions and large corporate culture that they don't notice those who are
no longer able to tread water. Many do not make it back to shore.

Is such random thinking and a "shot in the dark" approach by the adult
guardians of classrooms and schools a form of social injustice? Sure it is.
Social injustice transcends racial, economic, and intellectual groupings. Yes,
it is especially vicious to those who do not have privileged connections.
These kids too often feel not only ill-equipped to play the game, but they
are not even allowed in the game. But the disconnect between *any* student's
"heart of hearts" and his life at school, if left disjointed, leads to a lifetime of
searching and unfulfillment—a social injustice of the worst kind. The case
study below is based on a true story that hints strongly of a schooling model

that was broken, a schooling model that let a little boy just sort of wander away from the very passions of his life.

"I am sitting at my desk, forty years old, doing a job I don't like . . . have never liked. In fact, I hate this type of work. Yet, I have a family to take care of, my retirement plan forces me to stay here fifteen more years, and I'm probably too old to go chasing my childhood dreams anyway.

"But, I did have some exciting dreams. You see, from the time I was a little boy, raised on a farm in the hills of northeastern Kentucky, I have had a passion for nature, wildlife, the outdoors. I remember when my dad and older brother would take me fishing, or hunting, or back in the fields far away from the routine, I absolutely loved it! In fact, I still do. When I am truly being me, the unique one of a kind God intended for only me to be, I am not anywhere near this concrete 'prison' I work in. No, I am out in the woods in a tree stand, or with my son at a farm pond, or with my girls on a nature walk taking pictures, or with my wife sitting on our back porch right in the middle of a winter snow or a spring rain.

"As I think back, I most likely should have gone to school to be a park ranger, or conservation officer, or fish and wildlife biologist, or outdoor writer. But for some reason, not one conversation about my passions being connected to my future career ever surfaced in all of my twelve years of school. Oh, don't misunderstand. My teachers and coaches were good to me, I received a better than average education, and in elementary and middle school, I was in the top echelon of my class—making straight As and respected by my peers as one of the 'privileged' kids. In fact, if we would have a class reunion today, I most likely still would be. But, somewhere along the way, I got put in a box by the adults who looked out for me, and to this day, I've never been able to climb out.

"I remember dreading those bizarre speeches we had to give in class. I remember taking uninspiring, repetitive courses that I have never had to use one time since, although I'm sure they helped me in other ways—including being accepted into college, where I couldn't decide on a major that I truly enjoyed and thus finally escaped with a 'university studies' degree.

"And I remember ball game after ball game, as I went on to play baseball in college. One time, we were on a weekend trip to Alabama, it was April, we lost a tough game in the last inning, and on the long bus ride back to Kentucky I just kept thinking to myself, 'Where am I? Who am I? I don't even enjoy this anymore. What I'd give to be in the hills right now—with God, with nature, with that little boy that used to be me.'

"But how could I share these conflicting thoughts with Mom and Dad, who were sacrificing everything to help put me through school? I eventually became enraged, then disillusioned, as I thought back to conversations with teachers, principals, counselors—not even once since I was in fourth grade did anyone seem to notice that my true passion was the outdoors. Not one club was offered back then that would have satisfied my thirst to learn more about the fascinating world of nature. Not one time did anyone offer to take me to visit a college that had a major in my passion zone. Not one time . . . not one time . . . not one time!

"Today, I pull down more money than almost all my peers from back there in high school. And I am now putting my own kids through college. I have stayed true to the 'box' that others built for me, have conformed, have stayed within the lines, have made something of myself by society's standards. But every now and then, when I'm visiting a state park, or looking through an outdoor magazine, or reading an article on how to maintain a healthy deer population or how to make a dent in unhealthy coyote numbers, my eyes take on a distant look, and I wonder, 'What was I really supposed to do with my life's passion?' On those days, as soon as I can, I get out in the woods—where my chaotic world is then restored to order, and I am free . . . just as I was as a ten-year-old back on the farm, with my pony, the trails we explored, and my yearning to be one with nature.

"When I got married, my wife wanted to go back to school to study in the field of education. And let me tell you, I encouraged her every step of the way until she fulfilled that dream. Now, she's known as one of the best elementary teachers in our region. My two daughters want to go into ministry. Certainly not a profession that will pay them much money, but I am supporting them fully and cheering them on as only a dad can do, as I am so, so proud to give them my blessing to chase their dreams. And my son, a gifted athlete at his school, has told me he doesn't want to try to play ball in college. He's tired, perhaps even burned out after living on the ball field and at the gym since he was seven years old. I remember that feeling, and am embracing his decision.

"And me? When I look deep inside, I too have a dream. I have a dream that in just a few years I can retire, walk out the doors of this 'prison,' and never look back. I want to learn more about my passion . . . and I want to live it. And that is what I am going to do. I'm going to travel with my cousin to Colorado and hike for days, just like we started to do when we were young men fresh out of school. And I might just write about it. I love to write. Maybe I'll even land a job working in my passion. Oh my, I'd be in heaven!

"And secondly, I am going to volunteer at a school that is known for helping 'every child to know its name.' I want to be there for that kid who has no interest in conforming to the labels, and norms, and 'rites of passage.' I want to be a mentor to that kid, and look him square in the eye, pat him on the back, and say, 'What school do you want to visit? Come on, I'll take you. Let's go chase your dream.'"

QUESTIONS FOR REFLECTION

1. How does your school channel students to their "passion zones"?
2. Does your school's menu of student services allow flexibility for students to explore and engage in special interest areas? And in further independent study?

3. Does your school actively recruit club sponsors and content area consultants or mentors from the volunteer base in your community?
4. How does the staff at your school identify students who are beginning to fall through the cracks in regard to their plans for college or other post-secondary studies?

SUGGESTIONS FOR FURTHER READING:

Citrin, J., and R. Smith. (2003). *The 5 Patterns of Extraordinary Careers.* New York: Crown Business.
Gardner, H. (2006). *Five Minds for the Future.* Boston: Harvard Business School Press.

Chapter 14

My Kids

Before my children were born I knew what I would do when they misbehaved. Instinctively, I was certain that their misbehavior would be infrequent, that they would know and follow the rules. Nevertheless, on those rare occasions when they told a white lie or got caught in the wrong place at the wrong time, I knew exactly how I would respond and handle the situation. Then I became a parent.

Melissa and Karen were best friends. They were smart, cute, and loved to talk. Like many middle school girls, getting to class on time wasn't nearly as important as exchanging gossip with friends during the break or flirting with the boys. Their math teacher, Mr. Blatz, kept warning the girls that they were pushing the envelope, darting through the door just as the last echoes of the tardy bell was sounding. So, it wasn't too much of a surprise when the day finally arrived that the tardy bell sounded, Mr. Blatz closed and locked the classroom door, and began his planned lesson on division of fractions.

Scarcely thirty seconds into the lesson, a quiet knock on the door brought the presentation to a halt. It was Melissa and Karen. They began to explain, but no explanation would be acceptable. To gain entrance to his classroom, Mr. Blatz told Melissa and Karen they would have to get a note from the principal's office. As the girls turned to make their way to the office, Mr. Blatz closed the door, smiled inwardly, and returned to the lesson. Though he never let the students know, he could now brag to his colleagues during his next visit to the teacher's lounge. Melissa was the superintendent's daughter.

If you're an educator and have children, you need to expect that privileged thinking will impact your children while they are in school. Some teachers will give them breaks they shouldn't get. Others will hold them to a higher standard than they hold for other students. Few of your colleagues will be completely impartial when interacting with your children. And you will sometimes struggle when your role as a parent seems to conflict with your role as an educator.

When Ms. Jones, the school's disciplinarian, comes down hard on the class for what others would see as a minor infraction, how do you react, knowing your daughter cries herself to sleep at night, fearing Ms. Jones? In the past you would shake your head and complain, but just a little. Now it's personal. Or what happens when Jimmy, your youngest son, is placed in Mr. Scott's classroom, the weakest of all second-grade teachers? Previously, you'd assured parents and friends that Mr. Scott wasn't "that bad" and that their child would be okay. Now it was *your* son Jimmy. As you rush to the principal to get Jimmy's schedule changed, you remember words you'd spoken to others, almost embarrassed by your shallowness. It's okay for the other kids, but certainly not for Jimmy!

Their peers will assume your children get better grades because they have access to the tests, or at least conversations among the teachers that prove beneficial when grades are "given." They'll hear your children say something about the dinner that Dr. Insko, their AP history teacher, had at your house and automatically assume that he brought all exams and completed assignments with him. Many of their peers assume that all your children have to do is show up for class, be reasonably compliant, and they'll be "given" an A. It's somewhat like the "honor among thieves" syndrome. While their peers may see your children working hard, studying late, and going to tutoring, they are certain that your children's grades are determined more by *who* they are than by *what* they know. As a result, your children will sometimes rebel, purposefully failing tests and refusing to turn in homework, all to *prove* they're just like everyone else.

Todd's winning ways were a result of his natural athletic abilities and his father's drive to make him better. Todd was a champion sprinter on the school's track team and was nearing the school record for most touchdowns scored. His easy manner and sense of humor made him a favorite not only among his peers but among his teachers as well. He was college material. His father's expectations followed Todd off the football field and into the classroom. His study habits earned him a GPA of 3.97, third in the class.

Thursdays were always light-practice days, but this one was a bit different. The coach held back on the field, and all the teachers knew that with floats being built for the homecoming parade, there wouldn't be a lot of time for homework. With the track team and football team both blowing away the competition every week, school spirit was at an all-time high. Brandon, team quarterback, called out, "Todd, let's you, me, Tyrone, and Justin go for a ride before we head home." Todd hesitated, but just for a second.

Brandon pulled out of the high school parking lot and pointed his car in the direction of "the Lake." The Lake was on a farm owned by Justin's dad and was a favorite spot for the athletes to hang out. About a mile from school, Todd's phone rang. As he reached for his phone, Justin handed Todd a reefer. He took the reefer and answered his phone, "Billy, where are you? . . . Oh, okay." . . . We've just left the school and will swing back to pick you up." Billy was Todd's best friend.

Maybe it was the speed of the car. Maybe it was the officer's intuition. But as Brandon and his friends pulled back into the high school parking lot, Officer Dawson pulled in right behind them. Todd still held in his hand his cell phone and the reefer. Instinctively, as the car rolled to a stop and the boys saw the police officer, Todd threw the reefer out the window opposite Officer Dawson. It landed near the feet of Principal Barnes.

Without asking the first question, Principal Barnes understood the offense, had evidence provided by the perpetrator, and had the guilty party in his sights. Principal Barnes knew exactly the recourse he had to follow. This was the third time this year that he had found drugs on school grounds, and he was determined to make the campus as drug free as possible. The other cases had resulted in mandatory drug counseling and a semester's expulsion for each of the students. Should this case be any different?

The boys were on school grounds and Principal Barnes had the evidence thrown at his feet. A search of the car revealed a case of beer in the trunk and a bag of unrolled marijuana in the glove box. But these boys were "good kids." They were popular in school, usually made the honor role, and their parents were well respected in the community. Nevertheless, despite all that, perhaps the most difficult part of this case for Principal Barnes was that Todd was his son.

Good school leaders have a knack for making good decisions. They gather evidence. They see the big picture. They understand how their students think and the struggles that they face. They understand times when tough love is best for students, while other occasions call for decisions to be filtered by grace. They smile when parents say, "My children aren't perfect, but they would *never* lie to me." Sometimes parents understand the difference between the truth and the whole truth, but not always. When the guilty are their own children, even the best school leaders sometimes wear blinders or lose their sense of good decision making. Principal Barnes would soon be receiving a letter similar to the one he had sent to other families of students caught with drugs. The dual role of principal and dad was creating tension on the foundation around which his life was built.

QUESTIONS FOR REFLECTION

1. What steps should Principal Barnes follow? How involved should/must he be in the investigation and subsequent hearings? How is his relationship with his son impacted by this incident? How is his relationship with the rest of the student body impacted by this incident?
2. What is the role of the superintendent and assistant principal when working with Principal Barnes, his son Todd, and the other young men involved?
3. Should educators teach their own children? What are the pros and cons when your children are in the school you serve as principal? What can a school leader do to lessen not only the appearance but also the fact of privileged thinking when his or her own child is involved? What is *best* when being a school leader seems to conflict with your role of being a parent?
4. What is the impact on the children of school leaders? Is it fair that they are frequently treated differently by their peers and teachers?
5. In the first scenario, Mr. Blatz's smug reaction reflected deep-seated feelings about the superintendent. How was Mr. Blatz right or wrong in his reaction?
6. Is it true that as an educator, few of your colleagues will be completely impartial when interacting with your children? When you have children of other educators in your classroom, do you ever flinch when their children fail a test or you send them to detention for misbehavior?
7. Have you ever influenced your child's schedule to ensure that he or she wasn't placed in a particular teacher's classroom?

SUGGESTIONS FOR FURTHER READING:

Kidder, R. (1995). *How Good People Make Tough Choices: Resolving the Dilemmas of Ethical Living.* New York: Fireside.

Kirby, P., L. Paradise, and R. Protti. (1990, April). *The Ethical Reasoning of School Administrators: The Principled Principal.* Available online at http://www.eric.ed.gov/ERICDocs/data/ericdocs2sql/content_storage_01/0000019b/80/20/74/19.pdf.

Shapiro, J., and J. Stefkovich. (2005). *Ethical Leadership and Decision Making in Education: Applying Theoretical Perspectives to Complex Dilemmas.* Mahwah, NJ: Lawrence Erlbaum Associates, Inc.

Chapter 15

Rounding the Bases—Bring 'Em Home

Have you ever experienced, as an athlete or as a spectator, a game in which the bases were loaded but which ended without bringing the players home? Bringing even just one of them home would have changed the outcome of the game. The same is true when kids get close to understanding the material, but they have no one "batting for them" to bring them home. That is where we—as educators, as mentors, and leaders—come in.

Far too many students with average intelligence are not faring well in school. Many students with learning disabilities are not reaching proficiency. The bar to reach proficiency *is* within reach of these identified populations. There is no reason why 85 percent of students cannot reach proficiency if they have teachers who are vigilant and on watch, ready to connect the student to interventions the minute data indicate the material being taught is not being grasped.

Schools load the bases with students but don't always "bring them home,"—that is, oftentimes they don't bring them full circle. Teaching well but not getting good results is *not* teaching well. It does not matter how organized a teacher is, how well prepared he or she is, or how much he differentiates instruction. If he does not bring students full circle in understanding the material and being able to apply it, he is doing students an injustice.

An administrator once asked her teachers during a faculty meeting, "What is the lowest grade you find acceptable in your home with your children?" After much input the faculty came to a consensus that nothing below a C was acceptable. Many of these educators stated, "In our house, nothing below a B is permissible." The principal then asked, "Then why do we as a school allow our students to get grades below a C?"

Why not tell students that nothing below a C is acceptable? If they perform below that expectation, they will get an I (incomplete). Then, the mentors should provide an intervention structure that helps these students reach the minimal expectation of a C, if not beyond. This is bringing them home; this is bringing them full circle and bringing them *all* in.

The principal in this true story challenged the faculty. "Starting the New Year, after Christmas, let's make the students aware of the 'C or above' charge. Let's make students aware in advance that they will get an incomplete if they are below that. Let's inform the parents. Let's have strategies and a support system in place for students when they do not reach that bar. When you score a unit assessment, identify the students below a C or below proficiency. Give them an incomplete. Have them report to you in after-school tutoring. Re-instruct and re-administer that test or a similar one to determine if they reached the expectations."

The teachers struggled. Many questions had to be answered to put them in a comfort zone for this to happen:

- How many times will I have to re-administer the test to get the student to reach proficiency?
- What do we do with students who do not show?
- Do I get paid?
- What if I cannot stay after school, because I just had a baby?
- How will I get with the teacher who will have the student to inform them of the student's needs?
- Will the student get full credit or partial credit?
- If they surpass the minimal expectation, are we to give the higher grade?

Perhaps the most eye-opening comment came from a young, charismatic teacher who met with the principal after school to discuss his concerns with this "charge." His comments were revealing: "I feel like I am sacrificing my standards in allowing any student to come after school and after re-instruction at some point to retake the test. Period."

"Sacrificing my standards?" That day the educator and the administrator were at opposite ends of the continuum. The teacher felt he was sacrificing his standards to "bring kids full circle," to keep working with the students until the students "got it." As the instructional leader, the principal felt like she was *not* sacrificing standards in any way. In fact, she thought her standards were higher in that students were being held accountable to continue to work toward mastery. The charge was holding students accountable to "round the bases." Students were *not* off the hook, so to speak, until they reached proficiency. Teachers were held accountable to "bring the kids home," to keep working with the students, and to apply best practice strategies to help them reach the minimal level of attainment.

The teacher met with the principal five times over the course of a few weeks as he struggled with the charge. But he was loyal enough to follow through. The two had a strong teacher-principal relationship so he felt that he could come to his supervisor anytime to share his thoughts and concerns. On one occasion he shared, "The charge is *not* working."

The principal inquired as to why he felt that way. He shared, "I had ten kids who did not meet the minimal expectation, and only three showed up."

The principal asked, "How did the three perform?"

He replied, "Every one of the three who came met the minimal expectation or beyond."

The principal shared with the teacher that he was focused on the students who did not come in, pre-judging the program. She was instead focused on the three who came, adding, "We have a program that we can promote as 100 percent effective, if parents can get the student to the after-school sessions."

The rural school district found that offering transportation for after-school tutoring was too cost-ineffective. The students showing up were the ones whose parents had the means to get them to and from school. It most likely was not because the parents did not care to take advantage of this free service to improve their child's grade; rather, they just financially or logistically could not work it out. Who were these kids? High poverty, minority, migrant (and at other schools, inner city) kids.

As the situation played out, the principal continued to share with her teacher. "We brought three around the bases. Now let's talk about the other seven. Make a personal call home to learn what the issues are, and confirm that the issue is transportation as to why their child did not attend. Perhaps a few more will come as a result. Look at the list of seven students. Do they miss school? Are they here every day or often?"

The teacher followed the directions. Most, if not all, of the students rarely missed school. For some kids, school is where they want to run to, and home is where they want to run from.

The principal then shared with the teacher that he needed to create opportunities for intervention, support, and assistance during the day for those who could not come after school. Interventions needed to be timely and immediate, and she needed to eliminate or minimize the barriers that some kids faced, such as the lack of transportation.

"What about the kids that are just downright lazy and just choose *not* to do the work?" the teacher asked. "Should these students be allowed to come and improve their grade too? If kids think they can get a second and third chance to improve their grade, they will not try hard the first time."

The principal then asked the teacher, "Do *you* enjoy staying longer hours after school or doing something during school that, if you had done it the first time, you could have gone home at 3:30? Do you really think students like having a longer day? Perhaps if we get the message out that if they do not master the material, they are not off of the hook with a D or F, students will get the message of high expectations. We want students to believe that we will stay with them—and on them—until we bring them 'home.'"

The take-away message is, "Don't leave the bases loaded. Too many classroom seats are loaded with students who are close, but not quite there." Work to bring them full circle in teaching and understanding. Some kids can hit a home run all by themselves, but some kids need others at bat to bring them home as they have to stop at bases along their journey. Teachers and schools can work more effectively together to bring them *all* home.

QUESTIONS FOR REFLECTION

1. What programs are in place in your school that may be stopping short of bringing all kids full circle? What changes need to be made that could bring them home?
2. How do you feel about changing a student's grade to full credit if it takes extended time for the student to "get it"? What is at the heart of your school's philosophy?
3. What if your school gave students an incomplete and stayed with them until they reached mastery (instead of D or F)? What would it say about your school if *no* student received a grade below a C?

SUGGESTIONS FOR FURTHER READING:

McCook, J. E. (2006). *The RTI Guide: Developing and Implementing a Model in Your Schools.* Atlanta: LRP Publications.

DuFour, R., R. Eaker, and G. Karhanck. (2002). *Whatever It Takes—How Professional Learning Communities Respond When Kids Don't Learn.* Bloomington, IN: National Educational Services.

Chapter 16

Kids in the Shadows

Do you ever really wonder about those students that sit in your classroom, day after day, who never seem to participate or accomplish much? Some are painfully quiet, some are loud and boisterous. Nonetheless, they are with you, they are in your schools. If you only knew what many of these students go home to at night. It is an accomplishment in and of itself that they even get to school. They are passed by, outperformed by, and not pulled into the lesson by teachers who call upon the energetic few.

These kids live in the shadows of their peers. Many are just trying to hang on, hoping that someone will notice them, that someone will just ask why they are underperforming and passively "doing time" in the class-room. Many of these students are hoping that somewhere there is someone who can help them somehow pull out of the hole they find themselves in.

Who are your kids in the shadows? We must accept responsibility for these children in order that someday they can cast a shadow from the light that they exude.

Have you looked at the research on teacher questioning? You just might be surprised. As an educator, one would think that girls engage more in class discussions. Girls are more verbal, right? Their brains are wired toward linguistic intelligence. God only knows most females talk a great deal!

A middle school principal attended an eye-opening training once that challenged teachers to be more keenly aware of their questioning technique. The trainers encouraged the teachers to have their colleagues forgo a planning period to observe each other and provide "critical friend feedback" on their questioning. The critical friend was to note (1) which students were waving their hands to answer the questions, and who was being called upon and who was not; (2) the amount of "wait time" the teacher provided the students to answer; and (3) if the teacher "probed" the students for the answer.

The research surprised the observing administrator, supporting the fact that boys—Caucasian and middle class—are the ones that teachers call upon more frequently than they do girls! The same boys are repeatedly called upon. Little wait time is provided and little probing is offered to help the students answer the questions correctly. Thus, an injustice is done to the kids we leave in the shadows of the aggressive, competitive, high-performing eager beaver white males whose hands fly up the minute a question is asked.

The week following this training, the principal was scheduled to observe a topflight teacher. The lesson was well planned. The teacher differentiated instruction with various activities, and she was excellent in delivering the lesson. But it was classic. What the research said happened and what did happen was congruent. The teacher asked questions and the boys in the class waved their hand in zealous fervor to be called upon to answer the questions. The more the boys answered correctly, the more they were called upon. The girls, the English as a second language (ESL) students, and the low socioeconomic students were basically (but not intentionally) ignored. These students began to withdraw from the lesson with heads down and to exhibit off-task behavior.

At a break in the class, the principal pulled the teacher to the side and shared with her what had been shared the week before, at the training. She instructed her to ask questions, give more "wait time," and call upon other students. She told her she would tally how many boys, girls, and ESL and minority students would be called upon. She shared with the teacher that the aggressive boys may begin to show frustration that she was not calling upon them as often, but looking to others students. In so doing, the "passive others" might begin to perk up and become more engaged in the lesson. The principal encouraged her to move these students from the shadows into the forefront by providing them with a question, the pause, some probing, and then praise when they were able to answer the question.

The teacher followed the advice and the class was transformed in front of her eyes. Students that were not called upon previously began to sit higher in their seats. Students that were prompted or probed, and then who arrived at the correct answers, showed signs of improved self-esteem. These students began to raise their hands more in an attempt and eagerness to answer more questions. The before-and-after tally of student questioning showed marked improvement, as more students became actively involved in the day's lesson and activities. Educators often point the finger at the lazy student who "chooses" to withdraw to the shadows. Perhaps the problem is less the student's and more the teacher's. The problem that hinders learning can be something as simple as the teacher being more aware of the critical nature of questioning and the role that skill plays in student engagement in class.

That day the teacher in this true scenario learned the power all teachers have if skilled in questioning. She came to realize that, although she did not intentionally ignore certain groups of students, there were patterns of students not involved in the lesson. It broke her heart to see what the data revealed to her. She would often hear students make comments about how other teachers showed favoritism in their classes. She heard the voices of students who shared that "in Mr. So and So's class, I am a non-entity because of my color, my background, my status." It was at this defining moment that this teacher realized that she herself at times was perhaps one of those who made kids feel they were invisible in the room.

As a result of this feedback, the teacher became more aware of her questioning techniques. She became more able to pull students from the shadows by purposefully engaging all of them, therefore moving them from being passive participants to active, contributing learners.

QUESTIONS FOR REFLECTION

1. Observe a colleague and become a "critical friend," providing feedback on teacher questioning. Tally the number of questions asked, who was asked, and who was not called upon. Analyze the data. Are there patterns? Are certain populations not being called upon? Did the teacher provide wait time, and cue or probe?
2. How could you devise a means and process for being more aware of your teacher questioning tendencies?
3. How do you feel when you don't have an equal opportunity to share your ideas in a group discussion?

SUGGESTIONS FOR FURTHER READING:

Guskey, T. (1985). *Implementing Mastery Learning*. Belmont, CA: Wadsworth Publishing.

Raiche, J. J., editor. (1983). *School Improvement—Research-Based Components and Processes for Effective Schools*. Minnesota: Educational Cooperative Service Unit of the Metropolitan Twin Cities Area.

Chapter 17

Do You Accept Responsibility?

*What prejudices, what predispositions, and what history do you bring to
the table as a teacher or leader? Be honest. Everyone comes to the table
with issues, with a past and skeletons in the closet that oftentimes play a
role in how others are treated. If you can define what the skeletons are, it
is the first step in the process of burying them. You may say you accept all
children . . . but do you really?*

Emmaline grew up in the Deep South. If ever there was a Southern Belle, she
was it. She came from wealth and married into wealth. Teaching provided
her something to do and gave her life some purpose beyond cocktail parties,
Junior League meetings, and philanthropy work.

Her family owned a horse farm and considerable land in the middle of
Kentucky's Bluegrass. For over one hundred years, the full-time maid was
black. The gardener was black.

The migrant workers were a mix of Hispanics and blacks, all of whom
lived in high poverty. Emmaline's background knowledge was that of
privileged thinking. Because of this, as a teacher she favored students "like
her." She paid special attention to the higher socioeconomic status students.
Discipline was handed out in an inconsistent manner. Rules did not apply
to the student whose mom was in the bridge club with her. Bending over to
give needed extra help rarely occurred when the child had the stench of dirty
clothes and poor personal hygiene. Emmaline was not an ugly person. It was
just her background.

Billy Bob, the high school social studies teacher, on the other hand, grew
up in the country. Good ole boy Billy had his name engraved on his belt
buckle, and his license plate said, "Gone Fishing." To get a good grade in his

class, you had to be able to talk about fly-fishing, the statistics from the previous night's ball game, and trucks. If you wanted to talk about ACT tests and how to prepare for an Ivy League school, he referred you to the counselor. Chances are you got a B out of the class instead of an A, just because he believed that anyone who cannot talk about farming probably lacks common sense, and more than likely never worked a day in his or her life. And he resented that.

Ms. Annie, as she was referred to, was the art teacher. She was creative and brought the best out of talented kids. She had a penchant for students who expressed creativity and talent in the arts. She had little patience for students who had no appreciation for the elements of art. Either you had "it" in her class, or you did not. Students who performed well in her classes were often exposed to art in their upbringing, an opportunity more prevalent among students of privileged means.

Coach Furlong was just that, a coach. He was competitive. He was aggressive. He was a team player and team leader. Anyone who wanted to "go it alone" was perceived as different in his class, a loner. If you wanted to sit out, he would let you because he looked at such students as weaker individuals. He wanted all kids to be competitive. When you play, you play to win, not just to have fun. Games and activities in class modeled that. Games were fast-paced, aggressive activities that helped the strong get stronger and improve their skills, and that eliminated the weaker participants to the sidelines.

Two counselors roamed the halls. One was one of the football coaches. He advised the black students in the school to take "shop." Bruce, a high school classmate, once shared that he did not realize how black he was until his junior year in high school. This counselor-coach called him in to schedule him in the vocational classes in order that he could be better prepared for the world of work. Bruce could not understand why he was being tracked in this direction. Bruce was in all of the honors and college preparatory classes. The coach thought he was doing him a favor, as he was convinced that the chances of Bruce, as a minority, completing college and beating others out to land a job were extremely low.

The other counselor had a phobia for any students who entered her office that had dirty shoes, soiled clothes, and the possibility of head lice. After all, she had a sofa in her office for students to sit on—that is, students who had nice clothes, clean shoes, and well-coiffed hair.

Betty was a teacher whose pet peeve was poor manners. She constantly took students to the office who slurped food in the cafeteria. If students grabbed and snatched food like there was no tomorrow, she would take their remaining lunch and throw it away. She was taught by the etiquette book of Ms. Manners. She had manners, but she lacked heart. Who knew how many of these students whose lunch she threw away were longing to eat every morsel, as this would surely be their last balanced and healthy meal on a Friday, until school breakfast on Monday.

So, ask yourself: What predispositions do you bring to the table about students or a student's capability of success in your classroom? Do educators really accept responsibility for *all* students? The next time you have an unkempt student in your class, a timid child, an awkward child, or a somewhat poorly mannered child, teach them rather than berate them. You know not from whence they come. And if you really knew, you would not trade places with them in a million years.

A Prayer for Children, by Ina Hughs

We pray for children
 who give us sticky kisses,
 who hop rocks and chase butterflies,
 who stomp in puddles and ruin their new pants,
 who sneak popsicles before supper,
 who erase holes in math workbooks,
 who can never find their shoes.
And we pray for those
 who stare at photographers from behind barbed wire,
 who've never squeaked across the floor in new sneakers,
 who've never "counted potatoes,"
 who are born in places we wouldn't be caught dead,
 who never go to the circus,
 who live in an X-rated world.
We pray for children
 who bring us fistfuls of dandelions and sing off-key,
 who have goldfish funerals, build card-table forts,
 who slurp their cereal on purpose,
 who get gum in their hair, put sugar in their milk,
 who spit toothpaste all over the sink,
 who hug us for no reason, who bless us each night.
And we pray for those
 who never get dessert,
 who watch their parents watch them die,
 who have no safe blanket to drag behind,
 who can't find any bread to steal,
 who don't have any rooms to clean up,
 whose pictures aren't on anybody's dresser,
 whose monsters are real.

We pray for children
 who spend all of their allowance before Tuesday,
 who throw tantrums in the grocery store
 and pick at their food,
 who like ghost stories,
 who shove dirty clothes under the bed
 and never rinse out the tub,
 who get quarters from the tooth fairy,
 who don't like to be kissed in front of the car pool,
 who squirm in church and scream in the phone,
 whose tears we sometimes laugh at
 and whose smiles can make us cry.
And we pray for those
 whose nightmares come in the daytime,
 who will eat anything,
 who have never seen a dentist,
 who aren't spoiled by anybody,
 who go to bed hungry and cry themselves to sleep,
 who live and move, but have no being
We pray for children
 who want to be carried,
 and for those who must.
 For those we never give up on,
 and for those who don't have a chance.
 For those we smother,
 and for those who will grab the hand of anybody
 kind enough to offer.

QUESTIONS FOR REFLECTION

1. Be willing to be vulnerable and share a skeleton, or a piece of history in your background that may make you prejudiced about a certain population. How does admitting this bias make you feel?
2. Would you consider developing a survey and administering it to your classes to get a handle on how students perceive you? You do not have to share it with anyone, but you can learn and grow from it. Perceptions are real.
3. Has your school ever surveyed the student population as a whole about bias and prejudice that may be prevalent in the school community?

SUGGESTIONS FOR FURTHER READING:

DuFour, R., R. Eaker, and G. Karhanck. (2002). *Whatever It Takes—How Professional Learning Communities Respond When Kids Don't Learn.* Bloomington, IN: National Educational Services.

Sousa, D. (2001). *How the Special Needs Brain Learns.* Thousand Oaks, CA: Corwin Press Inc.

Chapter 18

Pecking Order

Tell a child she is good at something, and she will believe you and take that skill to a higher level. Tell a child he is weak, a troublemaker, or a loser, and he will live out your self-fulfilling prophecy. Send a message to a room full of children that some of them are the movers and shakers, and the rest should fall in line and follow the leader, and you have socially engineered the future of some of these kids who will indeed assume that they are destined to be followers, destined to be ordinary, and fortunate to join the worker bees outside the inner circle of the privileged few.

Mrs. Stinson was in her element, as dozens of her former students gathered at the school gymnasium to celebrate her retirement. She had taught sixth grade for thirty-five years in this community, and had had a tremendous impact on the lives of so many who had been in her classroom. As she sat at a table full of gifts and cards, she gazed around the room, reflecting on these, her most successful students.

Standing there by her side was Sallie, Miss Socialite. Mrs. Stinson had pegged her to be the class vice president, in charge of parties and other events, way back some twenty years earlier, and she was still playing that role in their little town.

Over in the corner were Luke, Bobby, and Fred, talking about sports, no doubt. Mrs. Stinson had called them her "all-stars," because they were such good athletes at such a young age. She had given them special places of honor in her class in their sixth-grade year, because she could see leadership written all over them, and wanted them to turn out okay—not wild and rebellious, a trap so many other of their classmates would most likely fall into later on.

And taking care of the master of ceremonies responsibilities was David, just as he had done in her class as she assigned parts for her annual sixth-grade play. David had a golden voice, and she had handpicked him from the first day he walked into her room.

David was chatting with Stanley, who had gone on to be the mayor of their little town. Stanley had been named class president the year he was in Mrs. Stinson's class, and she had asked the principal to send him to a leadership camp that summer. She could see politics in his future—even when he was twelve years old.

And working the crowd, making sure everybody had a good time, were three of Mrs. Stinson's all-time favorite girls—Mary, Samantha, and Brook. They were successful leaders in the community too, and she felt she had given them a good head start by doting on them way back when they were in elementary school. She called them "my girls."

Yes, it was a grand evening. A room full of adults laughing together, and praising the role model who had had a huge impact on their young lives by singling them out as future stars in the community. Mrs. Stinson had groomed them, so to speak, and they had not let her down. What a gifted and loving teacher she had been. She had cared for them in ways that went beyond the call of duty. And they revered this woman as she came to the end of a long and illustrious career as a school teacher—a molder of young dreams.

What Mrs. Stinson didn't notice, and it's good that she didn't at this stage of her life, was the huge number of her former students who were absent from this grand affair. Eddie, for example, one of her all-time troubled kids, was in prison downstate. He had actually received an invitation from the planning committee, but scoffed at the thought of sending a congratulations note to the woman who had kicked him out of the class play because he had not turned in the sentences he was told to write as punishment for chewing gum and being too funny again in class.

Eddie deserved the punishment for goofing off in class, and he never complained for being reeled back in when he got too loud or too silly. But he had never forgiven Mrs. Stinson for not letting him keep his role in the play. He loved "hamming it up," loved entertaining the other kids, loved being on a stage. He had even helped with the holiday programs at church, and was fascinated with the whole world of drama and telling stories through acting. But in middle school and high school, no one ever asked him to be in a play again. No drama club, no helping with props—nothing. So he had been in prison long before, being arrested as a young man for dealing in drugs, and being locked up at the state penitentiary.

Neither did Joanna show up for Mrs. Stinson's retirement celebration. Joanna had been one of the "in" kids in her elementary class, one of the most popular girls, who made good grades, had a great personality, and was liked by everybody. But in sixth grade, because she lived out of town and several miles from school, Mrs. Stinson had discouraged her from being one of the class officers, as the group would be meeting a lot after school. Joanna has never forgotten Mrs. Stinson's words to this day: "Really Joanna, how would you keep up? These girls do things together after school, on weekends, all summer long. They even go on vacation together. Don't you have another circle of friends in your home community that you could latch on to?"

And then there was Riley, or Willie Bob, as his classmates nicknamed him when he couldn't pronounce his name in first grade. Riley received the invitation, but he lived hundreds of miles away. He worked for a large magazine, and had made an excellent living as a writer. But Riley didn't talk much when in sixth grade. He was embarrassed that he still couldn't pronounce some words well, and back then there weren't many speech teachers. He already had the writing bug, but Mrs. Stinson mainly assigned homework that asked students to write about what they were studying. He was not inspired at all with this practice of regurgitating answers back on the page so the class could move on to the next chapter in the textbook.

Riley had held up his hand when Mrs. Stinson asked for volunteers to join her writing club at the beginning of his sixth-grade year, but she must have not seen it. Fortunately, in high school, everyone who wanted to could join the writer's club, and Riley enjoyed it so much he decided to major in journalism in college.

No, Mrs. Stinson didn't notice the many, many former students who did not feel any obligation at all to attend her retirement party. In fact, many of them probably never even found out about it, or had any special recollection of their sixth-grade year. This did not mean that they didn't like Mrs. Stinson back at that young age, or that she didn't provide them very dedicated support in preparing them for middle school. But simply put, there was not a connection beyond coming to school every day, and getting the work done. Mrs. Stinson did her best based on what she knew to do. And the kids did too.

After all, for most of those thirty-five years, Mrs. Stinson taught in a classroom with very little help from instructional assistants or volunteers. It was pretty much she and twenty-five or thirty kids—every day, every week, every year. So, by the very nature of the hand the system dealt her, she, and her students, operated under a somewhat haphazard game of chance, personality, and survival of the fittest.

Yes, Mrs. Stinson herself, and so many of her students over the years, were victims of the American schooling model that has sorted out children way, way too soon, and allowed this huge "crack in the floor" that does indeed result in many absences around the room at those grand and glorious retirement parties. Parties reserved for the select few.

QUESTIONS FOR REFLECTION

1. Does your school provide intentional training for all staff on being able to identify and support unique areas of giftedness in *all* students?
2. What is the process in your school for selecting the students who serve as class officers and in other leadership positions? For example, how are the students who put up and take down the flag every day selected?
3. Does your school have an array of club, cocurricular, and extracurricular opportunities for every student?
4. There are late bloomers and quiet but talented kids all over your school who are very capable of going on to very fulfilling careers and lives. But they are not in the traditional group of privileged students. How are these kids being groomed for future success in school and life? Does your school have a well-developed safety net for the students who are at risk of missing out on their dreams?

SUGGESTIONS FOR FURTHER READING:

Blanchard, K., P. Zigarmi, and D. Zigarmi. (1985). *Leadership and the One Minute Manager*. New York: William Morrow and Company, Inc.
Hatch, D., and S. Covey. (2006). *Everyday Greatness*. Nashville: Rutledge Hill Press.

Chapter 19

Elephant in the Room

How many times have you been a minority in a situation? Many of the more privileged have probably not fully experienced this in an entire lifetime, therefore they (we) cannot truly comprehend what that really feels like.

You may have heard for years that the "majority rules." What if you are not in the majority? What if your thoughts, your opinions, and your feelings are not shared by the moral majority?

What if the data you are looking at appear wonderful, but the data that include you, your child, your students do not fall in the majority? Would you look at things differently? Or do you look the other way, hesitant to spoil the celebration of successful overall scores—minus the kids in the gaps?

When making decisions, when developing policies, how do the decisions of educators impact minority populations in schools?

The fact that they are small in numbers doesn't mean that they are not living, breathing human beings who have the same dreams, goals, aspirations, and fears of the majority. If the squeaky wheel gets the grease, these voices make but a chirp.

Teachers and principals must be courageous crusaders who will be the voice of minority populations, and not be afraid to recognize and address "the elephant in the room."

What if your school's high-stakes test scores are above the state average, or even in the top 10 percent of the state, but only 10 percent of your 690 student population (69 kids) falls under minority populations (i.e., African American, ESL, etc.)? Upon further analysis of the data, your African American population and ESL population are underperforming compared to the rest of the students in the school. Who will put "the elephant on the table" and address the cultural deficiencies of these students, who are small in number but somebody's children?

Do you have the fortitude to say that you think the cultural mindset of the faculty and community is responsible for these kids' underperformance? Do you hear comments from the faculty from time to time such as, "Well, look at the names of the kids in the gap, look at where they live. What do you expect?" Or "Well, look at the data, these kids are on IEPs."

Poverty does *not* make one stupid. Being a student of color does *not* make one stupid. Being a student with limited English proficiency is *not* a reflection of one's intelligence or capability. You could be a Rhodes Scholar in Europe, but if you cannot speak French, how ignorant would you feel compared to how intelligent you know that you are?

Could there be an underlying culture of resentment that an increasing number of ESL students are in our country and our schools, requiring of educators extra work, time, and money to help these struggling learners?

Could it be a silent prejudice that teachers and leaders have of students of color? What we cannot comprehend, do we fear? A former physical education teacher in a K–12 school related the following story:

"Occasionally, as high school students would travel through the gym in transition to their next class these 'little kids in bigger kid bodies' would put their books down, and join with elementary students in a game of 'hug tag.' One memory however will be forever etched in my mind of what a student said while running past me with a beautiful little child running after her to tag and hug her, 'Get that little nigger away from me!'

"I was appalled! I was furious! I was speechless for a brief moment. I called the high school student over and proceeded to give her the lecture of her life. She responded with, "You don't understand where I am from! My family does not accept minorities. You will have to take this up with my parents." One of her parents was a teacher in this school.

"It was at this moment that I realized that people we come together with at school, in church, in our jobs, on the teams we play on, or in organizations we belong to do not all believe the same way."

People bring to the table all of the prejudices of their (our) past. These beliefs determine the decisions they (we) make, the policies they (we) develop, and how they (we) treat people. In your school, are there any "isms" that are the "elephant in the room"? Racism, classism, sexism?

A prism is an object that reflects and deflects light. The "isms" that negatively affect work in your school can many times be a reflection of a cultural mindset that perpetuates low expectations for these populations, which eventually allows them to fade into oblivion. Like a prism, the light that *could* reflect the beauty and talent of each individual student is perhaps deflected as people shy from being courageous crusaders in putting the "elephant on the table" and doing something about it.

QUESTIONS FOR REFLECTION

1. Describe a time when you were a minority in the room or your issue was the "elephant in the room." How did it make you feel? Was anything done about it? If something was done, was it of substance or just lip service?
2. What are the "isms" in your school? Can you list the "elephants in the room" in your school?
3. How can your school faculty design a process for addressing these brutal facts?
4. Substance (S) or Lip Service (LS): Consider your school. Put an S or LS before each of the following:
   a. _____You have a growing population of African American students in your school whose parents are vocal about the lack of support for their children to be successful. They are vocal that there are no minority teachers, thus your school hires an African American retiree to make home visits.
   b. _____You pair a stronger academic student with a weaker minority student in cooperative group work.
   c. _____Your school has many teams that need to practice after school. With the inception of girls' programs, numerous extra practice times are needed. Since the girls' sports were enacted later, the girls' teams start practicing from 5:30 to 7:30 PM. Lower numbers of girls participating is due to the fact that many do not drive and cannot come back later in the evening.
   d. _____You hire the first minority teacher with no support system in place to ensure success. The kids eat the teacher alive within a year, and the contract is not renewed. The reason? The teacher could not handle classroom management, often dealing with derogatory remarks as the first minority.
   e. _____A non-English-speaking student is coming to you in one week. You meet with the teachers and ask them to pair the student up with another ESL student. You encourage them to make flash cards, hand them a Spanish-English translation book, and tell them to go forth and teach.
   f. _____Do you have a policy that says students cannot invite a student from another school to a school dance? What about that 10 percent minority population? Today, interracial dating is more accepted by all

races. But some families—be they black, Hispanic, or white—would prefer that their child date within their ethnicity. Who do these small minorities invite or who are they invited by? What is your faculty afraid of in allowing them to invite someone from outside the school community? Have you looked at how many of your school's minorities do not attend these events? Perhaps you (we) have always thought, "They just chose not to come." Perhaps the elephant in the room is, "If you (we) allow them to invite outsiders, there is a cultural mindset that black kids cause trouble." These same outsiders occasionally pay to come to our ball games. I would venture to say that we are not escorting these kids from our games in droves.

g. _____You review school policies after you study feedback from student and parent surveys to determine if any of the policies are unjust to any population.

h. _____The counselor initiates a Knights of the Round Table group of students to address the growing minority population. Kids are involved in the development of and leading of advisory lessons that will serve as a bridge to a better understanding of cultures and ethnicity. The group also develops activities and events for interaction, dialogue, and celebrations.

SUGGESTIONS FOR FURTHER READING:

Johnson, R. (2002). *Using Data to Close the Achievement Gaps: How to Measure Equity in Our Schools.*

Patterson, K., J. Grenny, R. McMillan, and A. Switzler. (2002). *Crucial Conversations—Tools for Talking When Stakes Are High.* Columbus, OH: McGraw Hill.

Williams, B. (2003). *Closing the Achievement Gap.* Alexandria, VA: Association for Supervision and Curriculum Development.

Chapter 20

Culture, Community, and Consolidation

The lasting effects of school, other than the development of intellectual capital so one can successfully navigate through life, is similarly development of social capital. Humans are social creatures. Thus, kids need large doses of community, large doses of one-to-one and small group relationships, and large doses of making contributions and being valued by mentors and peers. However this happens, whatever formula is used, is not as important as the absolute necessity that this culture be indeed present. If not, chances are that a child can be in a schooling model for fourteen years, and, when he or she graduates, he or she still will not have a clue.

William's father seemed upset, as he finished the evening paper and began to read the school newsletter. "What's this about closing your school, William?"

"I don't know, Dad. I just heard some other kids talking about it at school. There's supposed to be a meeting, I think, for people from the community to share their concerns."

"Well, your mother and I are going."

A few days later, William tagged along as his parents joined about one hundred other adults in crowding into New Haven Elementary's little gym.

"Welcome everyone. We are glad you have joined us this evening as we gather info and make plans for our new school." The principal seemed a little nervous, and immediately several hands shot up into the air.

"What I want to know is, why are we doing this?" A middle-aged man in a suit pushed for an answer, and others nodded in agreement.

William's principal cleared his throat. "We explained all of this in an earlier session back in the fall. But I'd be glad to go over it again. Our school board has a window of opportunity in the next year or so to be awarded several million dollars for new building projects for our school district. But in order to realize this windfall, our district's facilities plan needs to be moved from planning to action. So, the board feels it's in the community's best interest to close our three small and outdated elementary schools, and move ahead with a large, state-of-the-art school campus that will house all of the students from the three smaller centers."

"So, that's it? To win a grant, you're closing three schools that have served our region for decades?"

"Well, not exactly."

"What do you mean? That's what you just said."

At this point, the board chair stepped in. "What we're trying to do is improve the quality of education for the entire county. Let's face it, the three schools in question are small, old, and without modern facilities. Is it fair to deny our kids the opportunities that other students have in the counties surrounding us?"

William's dad stood up. "Is it fair to take these pillars out of their local communities? Do you realize how long a drive it is from our end of the county to town?"

The board chairperson looked irritated, and cut him short. "Yes, obviously, we do. We've done all of the data studies, and it is clear that the advantages far outweigh the disadvantages."

William's dad didn't sit down. "Fair enough. If you will so indulge us, please list all of the advantages, and then let the citizens here point out the disadvantages. Seems that's the least you can do—unless your mind is totally made up."

The board chairperson smiled. "Well, to be honest, we do have an architect already working."

Suddenly, the superintendent of the district stood up and stepped front and center. "Actually, that's an excellent idea. Even though this is not our first public hearing on this, it would certainly be shortsighted of us to assume and move ahead too fast, without the input and support of our community stakeholders. If I may, I suggest that folks from the community stand and offer, one at a time and in a very respectful tone of voice if possible, reasons for keeping the three older schools. Then, perhaps we can roll out the preliminary model of our proposed new school, and let you see what could be a reality for your children within a matter of months."

One by one, parents from all walks of life and backgrounds stood and shared from their hearts what their local community school meant to them.

"I love it when I drop little John off in front of his building. I can park and walk him in, and someone is always waiting to greet or visit with me. And they always know his name, and what room he is to go to. There is a warmth and feeling of security I have as I drive away that I can't describe."

"I agree. It's not just a school. It's family. At Christmas, it seems the whole community is in that little building wrapping gifts, helping deliver food baskets. And the school plays the kids do every fall and spring—well, it's a tradition in our home that we have so enjoyed. Every one of my kids have been in those productions at one time or another."

"My kids love their teachers. They don't move around from class to class all day long. Instead, they bond with a homeroom teacher, and as the year goes on, it is very similar to when I was in school. The teacher becomes much more than someone who manages knowledge. The teacher becomes a lifetime role model."

"My kids love the principal. He knows their names, he has lunch with them, he goes on field trips with them. Sometimes he's even out there at recess, laughing and watching them play just to let them know he's not only about studies and grades. He's about kids being fulfilled and happy at school. I wouldn't trade that atmosphere for the world."

"And I wouldn't trade the advantages of a small school for the most expensive school on the planet. Over the years my kids have been involved in sports, band, chorus, any club they wanted to take part in, and have learned about leadership because in their little school everyone is expected to take on a leadership role of some kind. Can you promise that they will have these opportunities in a school three times the size? Won't the three ball teams we have now for each sport dwindle down to one? Won't the three yearbook staffs dwindle down to one? Won't the bands and the choruses dwindle down to one?"

"I'm sure your new school will have all the bells and whistles. And I'm sure the technology you can purchase with these available funds will be second to none. But, let me tell you—that doesn't matter if you throw away the culture for the sake of gadgets and more space. What good is it to have a larger gym if only a third as many kids get to be on ball teams? What good is it to have a beautiful, impressive building that resembles a mall, if in reality, the kids feel lost in the maze—as if they were indeed going to school in a mall?"

"My sister's kids were moved to a large, new school due to consolidation. She says it was the worst mistake their community ever made. The PTA is not the same: fewer parents are involved. The relationships between parents and teachers are not the same because the new school is too large and impersonal. And the students are so much harder to control. They are losing kids to other unhealthy interests. In fact, she's looking right now for a small school again that has the flavor of the former one that her kids used to attend. She says even if they have to move, that's what she knows in her heart she needs to do for her family while her children are in these critical schooling years."

"What about renovating?"

Everyone turned and stared at the back of the room. An elderly man with a cane was looking at the table of dignitaries. "Why spend millions of dollars, when you all could instead spend a few thousand on each school and bring it up to par with the modernization the state is requiring? And that way, you won't lose one bit of this wonderful formula these parents have described here. Be very careful, in your rush to please the bureaucrats, that you don't throw the baby out with the bath water."

The board chairperson's face turned red, as she explained that according to current regulations that would not be possible.

The old man simply added, "Little girl, if it saves money, I guarantee you there's a way to get it done. Put a package together, and I'd be shocked if the state officials won't give it a very serious look."

Swiftly, the superintendent stepped in and brought closure to the meeting, adding, "I sat here asking myself as I listened to all of your wonderful examples of the advantages of the small community school: 'Why would we want to tinker with the model we have now if we don't have to?' So, give us a few weeks to work on this, and we'll reconvene with you soon. Perhaps there is indeed a better way."

QUESTIONS FOR REFLECTION

1. How can your school, regardless of its size, better create an atmosphere of small community for each student in the building? What are you already doing well in the culture domain from the perspective of the student?
2. Why do you think so many parents do not feel as comfortable becoming involved in large schools?
3. Why do you think it is easier for students to get lost in the maze in larger school cultures?
4. Has your school district ever lobbied the state department to adjust its funding formula so it is easier to access construction funds without being required to shut down older buildings?

SUGGESTIONS FOR FURTHER READING:

Palmer, P. (1993). *To Know As We Are Known.* New York: HarperOne.
Wallace, R. (2009). *Breaking Away from the Corporate Model—Even More Lessons from Principal to Principal.* Lanham, MD: Rowman & Littlefield Education.

Chapter 21

You Brought a Dead Cat to School?

When rearing our children we were often told that kids will get your attention: either you find time for them through deliberation and planning or they will act out and, consciously or subconsciously, find a way to get you to focus on them. This is true, and most of us could cite many instances both from our personal and professional lives when this reality was evident.

Principal Ralph Holmes didn't expect Tom, an eleventh grader, to bring a dead cat to school—not at a time when, as principal of his third high school in as many districts and over several years, he was seeking to level the playing field and make the school a place for all students. And not at a time when he had actually gone out on a limb trying to free Tom and his group of about ten students from the grips of social injustice and the ramifications of privileged thinking—a culture that seemed to enhance the lives of certain students and incite inappropriate behavior from Tom and his buddies, all of whom dressed and looked differently, and who made most students and staff feel uncomfortable in their presence.

Before school, during lunch, after school, and whenever they got a chance, Tom's group wanted to play a game that most in the school did not understand. The other kids just assumed it must be inappropriate and just as weird as those who sought to play it looked and acted. Then it occurred to the principal that since the school was promoting student involvement in clubs, athletics, band, choir, and various other extracurricular activities, maybe upon closer scrutiny staff would find this game wholesome and subsequently begin a new club—complete with a faculty sponsor—for Tom's group.

To help him with this endeavor, Principal Holmes called upon Kelly Heather—a teacher of Spanish in her second year of teaching and about whom he had proclaimed the year before, "The best first-year teacher with whom I have ever worked!" She was very smart, caring, effective in her approach to teaching, and a strong disciplinarian. Principal Holmes asked her to research the game the students were playing to see if it was appropriate, and if so, give consideration to supervising them after school one day per week—with no additional pay—in conjunction with her Extended School Services (tutoring) responsibilities.

Kelly found out that Tom and his group were playing a card game that was, in her opinion, more like a board game because it involved strategy, forward thinking, intelligence, and quick wit. She thought it was appropriate enough for an after-school activity, although a little "dark." The game, according to her, involved "sorcery," power, and revenge until a winner emerges. She later provided some information taken from Wikipedia:

> Magic: The Gathering (colloquially "Magic," "MTG," or "Magic Cards") is a collectible card game created by mathematics professor Richard Garfield and introduced in 1993 by Wizards of the Coast. Magic is the first example of the modern collectible card game genre and still thrives today, with an estimated six million players in over seventy countries. Magic can be played by two or more players each using a deck of printed cards, or a deck of virtual cards through the Internet-based Magic: The Gathering Online or third-party programs.
>
> Each game represents a battle between powerful wizards, know as planes walkers, who use the magical spells, items, and fantastic creatures depicted on individual Magic cards to defeat their opponents. Although the original concept of the game drew heavily from the motifs of traditional fantasy role-playing games such as Dungeons & Dragons, the game play of Magic bears little resemblance to pencil-and-paper adventure games, while having substantially more cards and more complex rules than many other card games.
>
> An organized tournament system and a community of professional Magic players have developed, as has a secondary market for Magic cards. Magic cards can be valuable due to not only their scarcity, but also their utility in game play and the aesthetic qualities of their artwork.

The game played by Tom and his group was called "Magic: the Gathering." As a play on the game, they called themselves "MAGICians," as in those who played MAGIC, the game. Kelly classified them as "those lost in the shuffle because of their being just average. That is to say, apparently they had no clique (gamers, jocks, proud nerds, wasters, etc.) to belong to. They felt very lonely, unaccepted, and out of place. As a result, they did things to get attention, which made most people uncomfortable. They were underachievers although very intelligent, ignored the personal space of others, and spoke about topics that are typically avoided, such as the Columbine shooting, school violence, and death.

After she left the high school for a teaching position in a nearby county, Principal Holmes asked Kelly to comment on the time she spent with the MAGICians, and she said, "I think it's wholesome/worthiness was found in their grade improvements. They had to turn in progress reports *every week* to verify they had earned at least a C in every class. If they did not have a progress report or a C, then I obtained work from the teacher. Rather than play the game, they had to work with me, as their tutor.

"By the end of the semester all students (about 10 in total) were passing all classes with As and Bs. Additionally, I remember discovering that they were students who were very sensitive and hurt by how they'd been treated (and often I felt they had brought most of it on themselves and told them so, as our close relationship allowed). They were caring and very, very funny and, in short, just wanted a 'clique,' a place to belong to. They were treated differently, but I do not think low SES was a contributor, although it may have had something to do with it."

Now back to the cat! Soon after Kelly began meeting with the MAGICians, Tom brought a dead cat to school. Principal Holmes was confident that some of the naysayers, who thought Kelly's and his elevators were not going all the way to the top, were thinking, "I told you so! You can't help that kind of student! They will always take advantage of you! You'd better concentrate your efforts and resources on students who will appreciate what you do for them!" But neither Kelly nor the principal flinched! Tom was suspended from school for one day, but worse for him, Kelly suspended him from the group for two weeks (she met with them after school every Wednesday from 3:30 to 5:00 PM), and he was never a disciplinary problem after that. And as far as Principal Holmes knows, Tom was never suspended from school again.

Students at the high school level who have the characteristics of the MAGICians are often ignored or just tolerated. Life at school can become unbearable to the point that they either drop out, continue to be discipline problems until they are expelled, or sometimes do irreparable harm to themselves and/or others in the school environment. Truly, they are "tough nuts to crack." Yet, their humanity and normalcy can be brought to the surface if key people in the environment can find a way to positively focus on them, to give them attention, a way to show them respect and dignity while keeping behavioral and academic expectations high.

It has been said that no one rises to low expectations, and that students will rise to the level of expectations that their leaders set for them. This seemed to be the case here. A very strong teacher not only gained the respect of these students, but she also came to understand and respect them. She kept the expectations high, and the students worked hard to meet them. How much good would come about if more administrators and teachers in more schools would take risks in order to initiate programs and activities for the so-called weird kids, those who are not performing well academically, who never belong to any kind of school club or organization, and who—if left to their own devices—just may get everyone's attention in a most unacceptable and deviant way?

QUESTIONS FOR REFLECTION

1. Is it too much of a risk to invest time and staff to work with the kind of students who composed the MAGICians, particularly when their game was described as appropriate for an after-school activity, albeit "dark"? Explain.
2. Have you ever tried something special for such a challenging group of students? If so, how did your colleagues respond? If not, how do you think they would respond?
3. Evaluate the importance of having a highly competent teacher (person) working with students with these characteristics.
4. Think of MAGICian-like students in your school. Now list their characteristics and speculate on what you might do to get them more actively and meaningfully involved in your school.

SUGGESTIONS FOR FURTHER READING:

Wallace, R. (2009). *The Servant Leader and High School Change; More Lessons from Principal to Principal.* New York: Rowman & Littlefield.
Diebert, J. P., and W. K. Hoy. (1977). Custodial High Schools and Self-Actualization of Students. *Educational Research Quarterly,* 2(2) (Summer 1977), 21–34.

Chapter 22

The Indiscernible Faces of Privileged Thinking

So you think you could recognize privileged thinking if it were staring you in the face, huh? Maybe you can, but upon closer examination and reflection, you may not be the guru on this subject that you think you are. Up to this point in the book, for the most part, we have characterized middle- and upper-class students, parents, teachers, and administrators as the bearers of privileged thinking and the concomitant inflictors of social injustice. What if I told you that in the public-school setting, there are other contributors such as gangs, minorities, low SES students, businesses, special interest groups, and politicians who have an association with the schools who are at fault as well. Following are some examples. See how many are easily discernible to you.

Scenario One: Roy, after getting in trouble near the mid-point of his freshman year at the city high school, decided to avoid expulsion and enroll in one of the small county schools. He was from a broken home, stocky, quite smart (though at least a year or more behind grade level), and above average in height. When compared physically with the other fourteen-year-old freshman boys at his new school, he appeared to be a man among boys—and he did not hesitate to flaunt that.

"Let's trade punches!" Roy would say to any of the boys of his choosing. "You pick the spot!" was his next line, given in a threatening and directive voice, as if to say, "You'd better pick a spot or I'm going to smash your face!" The boys would always pick his shoulder, and he would always counter with a sucker punch to the stomach that caused most of them to double up, writhing in pain! Of course no teachers saw any of these episodes, or did they? No students ever reported any of these episodes, so nothing was ever done. The boys of the freshman class just tried to avoid him to the best of their ability.

Is it a social injustice for students to have to be educated in an environment where they clearly feel threatened and experience a sense of helplessness and despair? Do bullies practice their own form of privileged thinking?

Scenario Two: Before the first week passed after he assumed the principal's position at a large high school, a representative from a company that sold class rings to high school students asked for and received an appointment. Upon arriving for the appointment, the representative wasted no time giving the new principal a number of examples that showed that his company had never been treated fairly at that high school. He talked of how important it was for there to be competitive biddings arranged so that fairness to companies would result in quality products at competitive prices for students. According to him, the company currently getting the school's business had obtained it through "politics" and maintained it through favors to the high school and central office administrators. Fairness to students was never the top consideration, according to him.

Wanting to be fair, the principal did establish a committee of teachers, parents, and students, and arranged a competitive event involving three ring companies. As it turned out, the company of the representative making the early visit to the principal won the business (much to the chagrin of the company that had had the business for several years). The principal was proud of his committee, and even of the company representative who had initiated the discussion, because he felt a true free-market arrangement had been established at the school and that the students—*all* students—would ultimately be the beneficiaries.

Interestingly, four years later the principal under discussion became the superintendent of a nearby school district, which had one high school, and guess what company had the school's ring business? It was the company that had won the competition at the school where the superintendent had previously been principal! The superintendent was certainly content with this arrangement until two years later, when his son was a junior and it was time to order his class ring. And the rings were not cheap! The one his son wanted was around $400 and on the afternoon that the order was to be placed and accompanied by a down payment, the representative took his order, but not his check, stating that there was something he would have to check out with his father. The son complied, even though it occurred to him that the representative might have been thinking that his father would not approve such an expensive purchase.

Early that evening (of the day the rings were ordered) the superintendent did receive a call from the representative of the ring company—the same representative that he had worked with years earlier, and he had this message for the superintendent: "Your son came by with his ring order today and appeared a bit stunned when I told him that I needed to talk with you before I accepted his down payment and processed the order. The reason I wanted to talk to you, and of course I did not want to discuss this in front of others, is that I'm not going to charge you anything for his ring, just to let you know how much we appreciate your business."

The ring company representative was a bit shocked when the superintendent replied, "I don't want you to give my son a class ring. Are you aware that there is one family at that high school with triplets, whose parents have combined incomes equal to about half of what I earn? And if they can figure out how to get rings for their three children, I can find a way to purchase one for my son!"

The ring company representative was quite humbled by that experience and expressed remorse. He was reminded by the superintendent of his cry of foul play a few years back, and was told that no one associated with the school was to receive any favors, and that he needed to focus on giving *all* students quality products at a fair price.

How many businessmen and businesswomen working with schools are guilty of privileged thinking, expect teachers and administrators to think similarly, and therefore render a social injustice to the masses by driving up prices and/or providing inferior products or services?

Scenario Three: Why is it that all the students know that though their high school has limited restroom facilities, especially when there are just five to six minutes between classes, the boys' and girls' restrooms on the first floor are off limits to all except the African American population, which constitutes less than 10 percent of the total student body? That is the area of the building where the black kids congregate before school, between classes, and to some extent, after school. The adults in the environment are fully aware of this phenomenon, but no announcement or attempt is made to address it. The white kids just know that the black kids gather there, they seem to do a better job of sticking together than the white kids do, and if you enter that zone you will find it a very intimidating experience, so the best thing is just to stay away. Maybe you can get permission to use the bathroom after class starts!

Are groups such as the African Americans, Hispanics, gangs, jocks, and low SES students who congregate in various areas of the building, or school campus, guilty of privileged thinking? And do they render social injustices to other segments of the school's population?

Scenario Four: In introductory human growth and development classes, college students are often introduced to the concepts of mastery orientation and learned helplessness. Whether the terms apply to students in education environments, or their parents in the communities, the end result is often predictable. Those with a mastery orientation way of thinking believe that they are responsible for their own destiny. No excuses! Their self-talk is: "If I work hard, put in the time, work smart, then I can be successful. If I do not, then it is my fault. I have an internal locus of control; I am controlled from the inside. I am responsible for myself!"

Those students (or parents) who are of the learned helplessness persuasion take just the opposite view. Their self-talk is: "I am not responsible; I am the way I am because of what people (society) have done to me. There is no use in working hard; it will not matter. I will constantly be put down by the elite. I have an external locus of control; I am controlled from the outside. I am not responsible for myself. Furthermore, because others have put me in this predicament, it is their responsibility to take care of me! And finally, you can never do enough for me. Despite what you do, I will always be expecting more—grades, exceptions, no discipline when I violate rules, favors, money, benefits, and so on."

Are there really students in the nation's public schools who have what might be labeled a distorted view of privileged thinking emanating from learned helplessness? And if so, how could that result in social injustices for students, staff, and others in the environment?

Scenario Five: What about the funding levels for special needs and gifted and talented students? Regarding the former, schools have gone from a time when many with their handicapping conditions stayed at home or otherwise quit school at the age of sixteen or before, to the present day, when there is special legislation at the state and national levels that provide handsomely—in terms of fiscal and human resources—for them. When you look at the total student population in most public schools, you find special needs kids compose between 12 and 15 percent of that population. Has there been over-identification? And of this group, only a truly small percentage (maybe 2 percent) has severe handicapping conditions that unequivocally warrants increased fiscal and human resources for their educational program.

With current knowledge, can school administrators be certain that additional resources are needed to appropriately educate the vast majority of those identified as special needs students? It is not typical in schools for all classes for special needs students to average from eight to ten students. That may be necessary, even required, for the severely handicapped, or the students identified as emotionally disturbed. But would not the vast majority be just as well-off if classes averaged twenty students? Are there data to suggest that current practices are working?

Why is it that you could go back twenty years, ten years, or examine present-day practices, and find counselors and administrators encouraging students and others to pursue becoming a special education teacher because that is where the jobs are? This has led some to believe that anybody can become a special education teacher, and that special needs students would be better-off in larger classes and with the best teachers in the business. Does anyone really believe that the best regular math teacher in the school could not teach that subject to special needs students?

Could it be that parents of special needs students are guilty of privileged thinking, which has resulted in an over-emphasis and over-expenditure for the special needs population? Could this be analogous to affirmative action, which at one time was more relevant—perhaps a necessity—than it is today? Do politicians have the political will to openly and honestly address this issue?

Now look at the gifted and talented population, which constitutes about 15 percent—at the other end of the spectrum—of the total population in Kentucky's public schools (where students are identified in five areas as codified in both statute and administrative regulation). Kentucky Administrative Regulation (704 KAR 3:285) describes them as "students who are identified as possessing demonstrated or potential ability to perform at an exceptionally high level in general intellectual aptitude, specific academic aptitude, creative or divergent thinking, psychological or leadership skills, or in the visual or performing arts."

Similarly, the same KAR dictates that school districts employ a gifted and talented coordinator, and that staff "shall implement multiple service delivery options with no single service existing alone, district wide, at any grade level." Then eighteen examples of multiple service delivery options are actually spelled out in the regulation (such as cluster grouping, collaborative teaching, distance learning, seminars, special summer sessions, and independent study).

Though it is often said that more money should be spent on the gifted and talented student population—and to some extent the authors of this book will differ on this issue—isn't this emphasis on the gifted and talented a little too much? Since they are in the top 25 percent of the student population, anyway, in terms of academic achievement, athletics, leadership, and performance (vocal and instrumental, speech and drama, visual arts, and mock trial), can it not be said that public schools are serving, and have always served, this segment of the student population very well? Haven't these students always benefited from the privileged thinking of most stakeholders? Isn't this the population that schools have nurtured? Some have said that schools actually exist just for these students!

Is it privileged thinking on the part of parents of these students that has resulted in statewide and national associations for the gifted such as KAGE, the Kentucky Association of Gifted Education, which continue to lobby for increased funding and benefits for these students?

Finally, what is the role of the politicians when it comes to the special focus on a segment of the student population that seemingly has always done well, with or without specific legislation supporting it? Are most legislators from the middle class and upward? Is it their children who are apt to benefit? Is it the pressure from their privileged-thinking constituents that perpetuates the politicians' practice of providing special legislation for students who may already be getting a lion's share of the schools' fiscal and human resources?

At the beginning of this chapter, you were asked to see how many of the scenarios given were easily discernible to you. How did you do?

QUESTIONS FOR REFLECTION

Because the questions were couched in the chapter, no additional ones are given here.

SUGGESTIONS FOR FURTHER READING:

Bukatko, D., and M. W. Daehler. (2004). *Child Development: A Thematic Approach* (5th edition). Boston: Houghton Mifflin.

Kolb, D. A., I. M. Rubin, and J. M. McIntyre. (1985). *Organizational Psychology: A Book of Readings.* Chicago: The Dorsey Press.

Chapter 23

Learning the Constant—
Time the Variable

Competition is often good, but does it have to be so prevalent in our class-
rooms? Why is it not okay to tell a group of thirty students that they all are
capable of earning As in the course and that they all have a responsibility
of doing whatever it takes to help everyone achieve that goal? Why is it not
of great value to say to students, "In this class our purpose is to learn, not
to compete for valedictorian honors, not to determine who learns fastest,
or who is the smartest, but rather to ensure that we all work cooperatively
so that all can and will learn at high levels"?

What if all school faculty, staff, councils, and boards of education were asked
to support the concept that teachers must work with students and parents to
ensure that all missed classroom work, even if it occurs during unexcused
absences, is made up? When important work is missed, does it really matter why? Is not providing another opportunity for prescribed curricula to be
learned the compelling issue? It could be made up on students' own time; or
during time at school if it does not to impede the learning of other students.
In some cases this learning could be made up during tutoring sessions before
or after school, or even on the weekends.

In times past, and perhaps this is quite prevalent even today, particularly at
the middle and high school levels, students were not allowed to make up work
missed during unexcused absences because, very simply, it was thought that
teachers did not have the time to work with these students when they came back
to school. Teachers were still faced with moving ahead with the twenty-eight
students who had not been absent, and working with those who produced jus-
tifiable excuses for their absences. The intent (hopefully) was never to block
students from learning. Presumably, the intent was rather never to allow

discipline to prevent students from learning important curriculum. It was, seemingly, a matter of teachers not having the time, or the inclination, to help students master the learning if they had been absent without excuse.

And who was it that was more vulnerable, more likely to be negatively impacted by such an attitude regarding unexcused absences? Was it not the low SES, often minority student from a single-parent home who had very little support or encouragement, and whose parent could not readily secure a doctor's statement or otherwise meet the school's excused absence criteria?

While parents of students who already benefited from privileged thinking were quite adept at preventing absences from interfering with their children's education by quickly and easily obtaining appropriate excuses when they occurred, those students on the other end of the spectrum experienced perhaps the greatest social injustice of all: getting further and further behind in school because their absences were not excused. They received zeroes for missed work, and it is extraordinarily difficult to bring grades up to the passing level once zeroes have been assigned. This is virtually impossible for struggling students.

What if all schools had a goal of ensuring that 90 percent of the students would learn the core curricula at the 80 percent level of mastery or above? What if they made, beginning right now, learning the constant and time the variable?

Too often, time has been the constant and learning the variable. Students have been expected to learn what they could from 8:20 AM to 3:00 PM. Some learned a lot; some learned very little; some got As; some got Fs; and some received Bs, Cs, and Ds.

There must be a better way. In the past, too many students experienced academic failure. Those who needed more time or more opportunities to learn did not get it; too many students were not successful in school; and lack of success in school led to an unacceptable dropout rate.

If accurate statistics could be obtained, the graduation rate in this country would likely be less than 70 percent. What should be done when what schools are practicing isn't working? Shouldn't a different course of action be taken?

Schools should ensure that administering discipline does not block or prevent learning. Certainly, students should be disciplined because failure to do so cheats them; but staff should still come up with strategies to help them learn important materials, concepts, facts, and equations. Decision makers should devise a way to pay teachers extra for staying after school to tutor so that they can help students learn on the students' own time the important things they have failed to learn previously, whether that failure to learn related to excused or unexcused absences; or just because in the normal time allotted, between 8:20 AM and 3:00 PM, students just didn't grasp the required learning.

If tutoring is not an option, teachers should work creatively with parents to ensure that this important learning takes place. If it doesn't, students will get further and further behind. "The effective teacher," according to the late Madeline Hunter (1988), "ensures that students master one unit before going on the next." What a novel concept!

One way, albeit expensive for most school districts, to ensure that there is time for tutoring after school, is to get legislatures to pass laws making flexible school hours legal and enforceable. In other words, the school day would not end at the same time for all students. Because of present-day technology and the school staff's ability to immediately communicate with parents Monday through Thursday, if students should fall below the 80 percent level of mastery in any class, parents could be notified that the school day will be longer and that, for example, their children would *not* be on the 3:00 PM wave of buses, but rather on the 5:00 PM schedule.

If school districts could not afford to run two waves of buses throughout their entire geographical areas, then they could explore running them in the cities where many of the low-achievers often live, or in other strategically targeted areas of the districts. In many instances, parents, though impoverished, realize the importance of education in their children's lives and would pick them up after tutoring.

Having, for certain reasons, mandatory tutoring for all students, not just those more susceptible to social injustice, would have far-reaching student achievement ramifications as there are many students who do not make wise use of their allotted time during the typical 8:00 AM to 3:00 PM school day; nor do they always do their homework and assigned reading. What if they knew that with just a few clicks on the computer, their school day could be extended two hours anytime homework was not submitted in a timely manner, assigned reading was not done, or when they had fallen, for whatever reason, below the 80 percent level of mastery?

What if students knew if they did not get their work up to a satisfactory level through the regular five school days between 3:00 and 5:00 PM in tutoring sessions Monday through Thursday, they would be required to attend Saturday school from 9:00 AM until noon? Would they not get more serious about doing qualitative, purposeful, and intentional work during the regular school day? Would students not be more likely to do their assigned reading and homework?

Regarding mandatory tutoring, what if teachers knew that they would be handsomely financially rewarded for tutoring their own students—instead of sending them down the hall to a volunteer tutor, or of expecting parents to take them to a learning center not affiliated with the school, after school on Mondays through Thursdays and sometimes on Saturdays? What if *all* teachers took responsibility for the learning of *all* of their students? Other professionals do whatever it takes to be successful.

Teachers are professionals and if they were involved in a culture of high expectations, mandatory student learning, and fair compensation, they would do a better job of taking care of their customers (students and their parents) and would, literally, be offended if their customers sought another business, such as the Sylvan Learning Center (one of many remedial educational centers that has sprung up over the past few decades in the United States), to meet their educational needs.

When will teachers, administrators, parents, and board members fully grasp the concept that the purpose of schooling is to help students learn, and that it is important that they learn what has been determined as necessary for them to learn? When will these stakeholders fully grasp the concept that in all schools, the expectation is compulsory learning, not just compulsory attendance? When will they grasp the concept that the learning of the curriculum is not negotiable—it is not the variable, but the constant—and that time is the variable and will change as appropriate?

Whenever these concepts are sufficiently grasped, there should be inordinate concern about who teaches those students (mostly their own teachers, unless the principals and parents agree that due to extenuating circumstances, tutoring should be provided by a colleague), and that they are taught appropriately and given sufficient time to learn. The overriding issue will be that students be given enough time to learn the prescribed curriculum at the 80 percent level of mastery, or higher!

As a part of the strategy to help struggling students grasp prescribed and important material, particularly when it occurs during unexcused absences, schools must find better ways than the assignment of zeroes. One way to do this would be to assign quality points to grades as is done in college, with an A receiving four points down to an F receiving zero quality points. Forget about makeup work and tutoring right now and think of a student who misses an assignment and is given zero quality points (an F). On the next assignment, he receives a B, three quality points. The three points divided by the two assignments equals 1.5 quality points—a C– average on the two assignments.

Now consider the 100-point system, and the student who misses an assignment gets a zero, but then makes an 80—a B on the next assignment. These 80 points divided by the two assignments equals an average of 40, still at least 20 to 25 points below a passing grade of 60–65 in most schools.

A second strategy in combating the ill effects of the zero would be to always assign a 59 (or maybe even a 50) if the passing score in the school is

60, or 64 if it is 65, to any missed or substandard work. The student still gets an F for such, but is not put behind the eight ball, not put in what appears to students—and to many well-informed observers—as a nearly impossible hole from which he must attempt to climb out. When hope is lost, many students, especially the disenfranchised, those bearing the brunt of privileged thinking and social injustice, will give up and not make the effort that most of us would take for granted.

In conclusion, by making learning the constant and time the variable, being creative in finding more time for students to learn, arranging for teachers to receive fair compensation for appropriately teaching and tutoring their own students, and developing strategies to combat the ill effects of the assignment of zeros, all learners, and in particular those most susceptible to social injustice, will be favored.

QUESTIONS FOR REFLECTION

In this chapter, as a way of engaging the reader and presenting main ideas, many questions were provided. Some were rhetorical, and some were asked and answered, but perhaps not as you would answer them. In your small groups, and as time permits, start at the beginning of the chapter and provide your answers to the questions.

SUGGESTIONS FOR FURTHER READING:

Hughes, R. (2003). *The Educational Good News for Hardin County Schools.* A compilation of research for district use, Elizabethtown, KY.

Edmonds, R. R. (1981). Making Schools Effective. *Social Policy,* 12(2) (September–October 1981), 56–61.

Chapter 24

More Equal than Others

No one believes more firmly than Comrade Napoleon that all animals are equal. He would be only too happy to let you make your decisions for yourselves. But sometimes you might make the wrong decisions, comrades, and then where should we be?

—Squealer (from *Animal Farm*)

As a high school sophomore, James remembers grumbling about having to read *Animal Farm* to satisfy his English teacher, Mr. Sinnet's, misplaced passion for this strange, but popular with literature teachers, novel. The class discussed its plots and subplots, the protagonist and followers, the surface message, and what the author was *really* trying to say. (James wondered why authors just don't *say* what they mean without requiring the reader to think.) But as years have passed James has been surprised by his recollection of many of the more salient points of *Animal Farm,* especially the "Seven Commandments of Animalism."

The book's readers will remember that the animals took over the farm from an often-drunk Mr. Jones in an effort to improve their living conditions and exist together in harmony. To accomplish this task, a list of rules or commandments was developed.

Seven Commandments of Animalism
1. Whatever goes upon two legs is an enemy.
2. Whatever goes upon four legs, or has wings, is a friend.
3. No animal shall wear clothes.
4. No animal shall sleep in a bed.
5. No animal shall drink alcohol.

6. No animal shall kill any other animal.
7. All animals are equal.

For a while harmony prevailed on the farm until some of the animals, specifically the pigs, found it expedient to change some of the command-ments. The fourth commandment was changed to "No animal shall sleep in a bed *with sheets.*" The fifth was changed to "No animal shall drink alcohol *to excess.*" The sixth to "No animal shall kill any other animal *without cause.*" And the seventh commandment was changed to "All animals are equal, *but some animals are more equal than others.*"

It is the change in the seventh commandment that captures the attention of many because its application is pervasive in many of today's schools and defines much of what we understand about privileged thinking. Consider the following case:

Dr. Buel, a recently retired superintendent, was asked to conduct an inves-tigation in a district where a superintendent planned to dismiss a tenured teacher. Many people equate tenure with a life contract, and for all practical purposes, the two are nearly equal. Nevertheless, effective school leaders confront mediocrity head-on. A retiring principal, one who had sometimes ignored mediocrity, yielded a change in administration. The new principal knew that accepting the status quo was not best for students.

It wasn't too many months into the school year when the new principal realized that one of her veteran teachers, Ms. Bailey, was at best a marginal English teacher. While Ms. Bailey knew her content, she often bullied the students, engaging in verbal free-for-all's that led to loss of class time. Parents complained. Students complained. The principal and teacher confer-enced. Little changed. Components of improvement plans were often ignored and led to no lasting improvement. The principal kept the superintendent informed, who eventually accepted the principal's recommendation to dis-miss Ms. Bailey. Believing that a court case was looming, the superintendent asked Dr. Buel to investigate and provide a professional opinion. Would the facts of the case stand up in court?

It was a rather large school, and Dr. Buel began his investigation with indi-vidual interviews with other members of the English department. Dr. Buel's first question was, "Please tell me the professional strengths of Ms. Bailey." The most frequent comments focused on knowledge of content. Ms. Bailey knew the important components of English. "Are her instructional strategies effective to help students learn these important components?" Dr. Buel contin-ued. The most frequent initial response to this question was eyes darting from one side to another, a reaction that many have when they don't want to say the first thing that comes to their mind. Most of the English faculty members tiptoed through the minefield of potential responses to this and subsequent questions. The last question Dr. Buel asked of each of Ms. Bailey's colleagues was, "On the first day of school, if your child came home from school and you learned that he or she had been assigned to one of Ms. Bailey's classes, what would you do?" The unanimity of responses to this question was amazing. *Every one* of Ms. Bailey's colleagues said, "I would do what I needed to do to get my child's schedule changed." And, two continued, "If I couldn't get the schedule changed, I would withdraw my child from school."

This was Ms. Bailey's seventeenth year as an English teacher. Many of her colleagues had worked with her all of those years. While it was *not* acceptable for Ms. Bailey to teach the faculty's children, it seemed that it had been okay for Ms. Bailey to teach many other children for seventeen years. Apparently, in this school, some children were more equal than others. Why would any educator think it's okay for *some* kids to have mediocre or poor teachers, but not for their own?

As educators you no doubt have noted several school policies that have been adopted for any number of reasons. Most of these are well intentioned and, when enforced consistently, seem to be effective. However, when inconsistent implementation reigns, one can bet that the notion that some children are more equal than others (a.k.a. privileged thinking) is a part of the school's culture. Do any of these seem familiar?

Rule: *No students allowed in the faculty/staff lounge.*

The faculty/staff lounge can be a bastion of relaxation or a cesspool of gossip and innuendo. The difference is determined by the professionalism, skill, and culture found within the school. Frequent conversation can be overheard about particular students, their behaviors, and academic abilities. It's wise when a rule has been established that no students should be in the lounge. But having seen this rule posted on most faculty/staff lounges, in practice it seems to mean, "No students allowed in the faculty/staff lounge *unless you're a child of a faculty/staff member.*"

Why is it okay for Teacher Smith's child to drink soft drinks from the ever-present soft drink machine and frequently overhear adult conversations about other students, when Farmer Jones's child does not have that access? In actuality, the rule is appropriate. It's the inconsistent enforcement of that rule that is problematic.

Rule: *In order to participate in an after-school activity, a student must be present at school for the entire day.*

Thomas Reynolds High School was having trouble with students staying at school on the day of the prom. Girls wanted to leave at noon the day of the prom to make that one last trip to the tanning bed and to sit in the beautician's chair in order to attain just the right look. To eliminate the problem, the school council adopted the above policy, and for the prom it seemed to solve the problem. Typically, proms occur near the end of the school year, and the implications of strict adherence to the rule were not apparent until the following fall.

When school resumed in the fall a number of other activities also started—football, track, cheerleading, speech club. The day of a home track meet, the school's best cross-country runner had a doctor's appointment. Two weeks later the lead tackle attended his grandfather's funeral the afternoon of the homecoming game. The following Monday, the speech team was hosting an invitational tourney. Twins on the debate team had a father who was being recognized at the state capital for his work with the local recycling efforts.

The fervor over the policy grew with surprising speed and the council responded by revising the rule to read, "In order to participate in an after-school activity, a student must be present at school the entire day *unless prior approval is granted by the school principal.*" The change seemed reasonable—after all, the students represented in the three previous examples weren't missing school to have their hair fixed or to go to the tanning bed. And principals should have discretion to consider all aspects of a situation in order to make a professional decision. But there are times when exceptions are made for the lawyer's son or the doctor's daughter, and not for the farmer's or janitor's children.

Unwritten Rule: *The needs and wishes of the faculty supersede the needs of the students.*

Why is it that the football coach or the band director has planning period the last period of the day? Why are the veteran teachers often assigned the most advanced students with the fewest discipline problems? Why aren't classroom assignments changed (e.g., moving Mr. Smith from room 23 to room 56) unless Mr. Smith retires? Too often the needs of the adults trump the needs of the students.

The reader should not misunderstand. Teachers give and give and give. There should be perks for teachers. Teachers' needs and desires *must* be considered. Teaching is a high calling and those who choose this profession should be honored. *But* when these considerations interfere with making the best decision for students, the most effective educators will come down on the side of the students. In some schools, the needs of the students always come *after* the needs of the adults in the building.

Are there times in our schools when some students *are* more equal than others? Does equal and equitable treatment mean the same thing? When a student with dyslexia is provided assistance to complete a test, does that mean this student is more equal? When the parent of a student comes back from overseas deployment on the day of the prom, if the student greets her father at the airport at noon and attends the prom that night, does that mean this student is treated more equal than others? When the student with a broken leg parks in the teacher's parking lot, is this student more equal than his classmates?

As I write this chapter I'm on a flight from Orlando to Cincinnati, sitting in first class. While I don't often travel, when I do, my bank account never allows me to sit in first class. But this morning, while I was waiting to board the plane, the agent at the gate announced, "I have some first class seats available for anyone in coach who would like to upgrade. The cost is $75." I don't know whether it was my weariness from the three-day meeting that I had just attended or the day-old, slightly tangy apple juice I had had for breakfast, but the notion of sitting in first class on my way home was too much to resist. Though $75 doesn't come easy to my bank account, I was committed.

So, here I sit on a plane with over one hundred passengers. Fourteen of us are more equal than others. We have larger seats, better food, and certainly more attention from the flight attendants. Did we pay for the extra service? Certainly. But I wonder if some of our students believe they deserve to be treated more equal because they've paid with their intellect, or athletic ability, or their singing voice, or their ancestry, or their academic aptitude.

In some schools these qualities do equate to a prevailing practice according to which some students are considered more equal than others. Over the course of time, these practices become the norm, and the more equal students (and very often their parents) come to see the treatment as a right in all aspects of schooling. When unequal treatment is consistently provided to equals, this practice becomes problematic.

My first class experience is soon coming to an end. To be honest, I've enjoyed being more equal than most of the other passengers during the last couple of hours. I suspect students who find themselves the recipients of privileged thinking also enjoy the experience. Now, I just have to figure out how to tell my wife about the $75 expense on our charge card.

QUESTIONS FOR REFLECTION

1. Does equal treatment and equitable treatment mean the same thing? Is it okay at times to give some students an advantage when completing tasks similar to others?
2. What are perks that should be enjoyed by teachers? Do these perks ever interfere with making the best decisions for students?

3. Have you ever been treated more equally than others? How did you feel? Did you feel that you earned it?
4. Have you ever been treated less equally than others? How did you feel? Did you feel that you earned it?
5. Some parents will *always* feel that children of other parents are given special treatment. How do educators fight this perception? Are there instances in your school where this perception might be warranted?

SUGGESTIONS FOR FURTHER READING:

Clare, E. (2003). *Digging Deep: Thinking about Privilege.* Retrieved February 3, 2010, from http://eliclare.com/what-eli-offers/lectures/privilege.
Orwell, G. (1954) *Animal Farm.* New York: Harcourt Brace.

Chapter 25

The Kids Say I'm Black

The words of the late singer Michael Jackson should ring loud and clear from his song "It Doesn't Matter If You're Black or White." *But it still does. Why does being either black or white create mental models of something positive or negative? Give all kids a chance. Teach people to give others a chance.*

An elementary PE teacher was faced with a crying second grader entering the gym. The child was just boohooing. She was a cutie bug. Her skin was golden brown, her eyes a sparkling sea-green. On most days, she bounced into the gym with a wide, toothless smile to match! Usually, she came running up to the PE teacher with a hug. Today, she desperately needed one.

Apparently back in the classroom, Cindy was filling out one of those student data reporting system forms. She was asked the question of race. The classmates around her told her that she had marked hers wrong. They told her she was black.

Cindy was shocked, hurt, devastated—and she began to cry. She denied to her classmates that she was black and she was mad at them for saying so.

The teacher was at a loss in how to address the situation. You see, Cindy's mom was white. Her mom never married, and Cindy never met her dad. Her grandparents and cousins, aunts and uncles were all white. No one ever said anything to the contrary to her.

Is Cindy black . . . or white? Why is it important that she be either? Why does that matter? Why did this small child associate being black with something negative? If your teacher said your heritage was Italian, would you cry? If someone said your ancestors came from Virginia, would that devastate you? Why was a piece of this child's innocence lost on that Monday morning at school?

Cindy went from being a happy-go-lucky child of seven to a child that did not like what she saw in the mirror. Her classmates responded to her in a childlike manner, blatantly blurting their ignorance out to her. Yet, why did they think it was a big deal to tell her that information? They knew enough in their innocence that some frowned on black students, especially in this predominantly white school. The students told her because they knew it would hurt her. Kids can be so loving and then so cruel in a matter of seconds. They demonstrated the epitome of being "culturally insensitive."

Most, if not all, of the children in the class could probably not verbalize why they thought being black was bad, or why it seemed like something for which to make fun of Cindy. Life more than likely had not taught them about the injustices that minorities sometimes face. But they knew enough that she was different.

How many times have "teachable moments" such as this—excellent opportunities to educate about diversity—been ignored in the classroom? Better yet, how many teachers intentionally plan and teach acceptance and diversity before a crisis arises?

QUESTIONS FOR REFLECTION

1. Share one example of how you have designed lessons or activities to address a diverse student population. Does your school emphasize this core value in developing curriculum?
2. Analyze your school's culture. Would you say that the school is sensitive to minority groups in the school? How? How not? If not, how can the school address the deficiencies?
3. Let's say your school or district's minority population is very low. Do you still provide instruction on cultures that are different from your own? If you do not, how are you preparing your students for the culturally diverse society in which they will live? Statistics tell us that by 2020 the U.S. population will be 40 percent Hispanic. Discuss.

SUGGESTIONS FOR FURTHER READING:

Gay, G., and J. Banks. (2000). *Culturally Responsive Teaching: Theory, Research, and Practice.* New York: Teachers College Press.

Jenkins, W. (2004). *Understanding and Educating African American Children—Excuses to Excellence.* St. Louis, MO: William Jenkins Enterprise.

Ladson-Billings, G. (1997). *The Dreamkeepers: Successful Teachers of African American Children.* San Francisco: Jossey-Bass.

Chapter 26

We Are *All* Gifted, and We *All* Have Disabilities

There is more that makes us similar than that which separates us.

We all have areas of strength and areas of weakness. The areas of talent need to be cultivated as much as the areas of deficiency need to be provided interventions for. When schools do not provide this equal opportunity, the educational system is doing an injustice to students. Legislators and political entities need to begin to address more intentionally the gifted and talented students by dedicating financial support in the areas of human resources (more teachers addressing gifted and talented issues), and the need for more time to meet these students' needs. Is anyone out there developing GRTI (Gifted Response to Intervention)?

An administrator of approximately seven hundred students in an inner-city high school had eight teachers on staff hired full-time to address the needs of students with disabilities Monday through Friday. Educators know the routine: these students are tested, identified, and placed. Federal monies are allocated to pay for the teachers and the resources needed to help these identified students meet, and possibly exceed, state academic standards.

In contrast, one itinerant teacher was assigned to the same school one day a week to address the needs of the gifted (identified) student population. Federal dollars paid for the teacher and the resources.

At this school, the numbers of identified students in special education and those identified as gifted were almost identical. What is wrong with this picture in a country that wants to remain competitive in a global economy? It is not that special education students need less so as to afford the gifted students more; they all need equal emphasis and ongoing support for their unique needs.

A first-year assistant principal shared that she recognized the problem early on. Her principal and mentor tried to explain why it is what it is. He had her visualize Jimmy, one of our special education students who had Down's syndrome. Jimmy came from a middle-class family and was as sweet as they come. He was a hugger who went around school lifting everyone's spirit with compliments and a smile a mile wide. He had an eternal childlike spirit. He was a gift to all who had the pleasure of knowing him. But it was obvious that Jimmy and the teachers who worked with him would need extra resources to meet his needs.

The mentor then asked the young assistant principal to visualize Tyler. Tyler was from an upper-middle-class family. He came to school wearing the button down shirt, khaki pants, and loafers. He was articulate, handsome, sharp, and gifted.

Now picture both of them standing in front of legislators on the floor of the Senate in front of a microphone. Jimmy would smile and stutter and stammer and tug on the emotion of everyone in the room. In fact, there may not be a dry eye in the room when he is done. Tyler, on the other hand, would take to the podium like a budding politician with all the confidence and a swagger that would match, if not exceed, that found in the room. Where do you think legislators are going to put their money? Who has the greatest need?

This country has a need to help and nurture our best and our brightest. This country has an alarming need to address a growing apathy of status quo and acceptance of mediocrity as the norm.

Yes, Jimmy *may not be* self-sufficient beyond minimal community-based life skills. Yes, Tyler is a survivor with resources to help him take flight. But how high could Tyler fly, and gifted kids like him, if they were provided with equal opportunities and resources to meet their needs? It's past time that schools stop simply wondering about it, and instead *do something* about it. The clock is ticking for these students and for our country.

QUESTIONS FOR REFLECTION

1. When was the last time legislators spent some quality time *in* the schools in your district to see what *is* or is *not* being offered our gifted students?
2. Student voices are powerful. Poll gifted students and inquire about how they feel their needs are being met, or not. What common frustrations do you predict they will share?
3. When was the last time you as a teacher or you as an administrator made contact with a legislator or a lobbyist? The collective voices of the

professionals doing the work are powerful as well. Be encouraged to not sit back in hopelessness, but rather step to the plate and be heard.

SUGGESTIONS FOR FURTHER READING:

Armstrong, T. (1998). *Awakening Genius in the Classroom.* Alexandria, VA: Association for Supervision and Curriculum Development.

Slocumb, P., and R. Payne. (2000). *Removing the Mask—Giftedness in Poverty.* Highlands, TX: Aha Process, Inc.

Tomlinson, C. (2001). *How to Differentiate Instruction in Mixed Ability Classrooms.* Upper Saddle River, NJ: Prentice Hall.

Chapter 27

Closing Thoughts

We Can Do It! We Must Do It!

I dreamed of a better day for my children and my grandchildren when all children are granted equal and equitable opportunities to learn. From the moment I dared to think it, it started coming true. And I never gave up on the dream—not for one day.

Just suppose a school full of kids and their teachers were given the opportunity to design their dream school of the future, devoid of social injustice. Politicians, special interest groups, and the restraints and paradigm lock of the bureaucracy would stay out of the way, and all the details of this new state-of-the-art and *state-of-the-heart* learning center would be left to those who would actually manage it, live in it, and study in it. Wow, what a novel thought. Almost seems too good of an idea to take seriously, doesn't it? But let's just indulge ourselves in dreaming for a few moments. What would such an endeavor lead to? What would begin to take shape? What would be the end result of such creative, outside-the-lines, unchained thinking?

Students would quite possibly offer ideas such as:

Let's have more experiential learning, and not so much sitting in seats all day long.

Let's not be driven by bells and rigid schedules.

Let's have more fluid and natural activities and class time that is not so packaged and artificial.

Science class needs to have lots of lab time.

Reading needs to be something we enjoy, so take the time to make sure we can read.

We will write creatively if you help us with it and give us time to do it.

It is a unique teacher who can teach math well. Without that, we're lost in math.

Can we ease up on the endless tests?

Please don't put us with teachers who don't want to be here.

We've grown up on technology. Please let us use it as a key part of our learning process.

Respect us for who we are, and help us develop into who we can be.

If we seem bored, it's because often we are bored.

Actually, we like it when our classes are challenging.

Help us be ready for life after high school.

Help us to navigate through the maze of paperwork and scholarship applications.

Help us with "real life" skills.

Be real with us, talk to us, get to know us, communicate with us.

We need mentoring and steering. We don't need yelling, sarcasm, belittling.

The more clubs and bonus activities the better. School is so much more than class time.

We love guest speakers, career days, health fairs, field trips, work studies, and shadowing.

We love trips to farms, the outdoors, and a variety of PE and recreational opportunities.

We're into sports. We're not into treating athletes as superior to the rest of us.

We're also into art, music, drama, guitar lessons, band, and chorus. Remember that.

We actually will pitch in on community projects and visit senior citizen homes.

We like internships, taking classes online, and taking college courses when we're ready.

We don't get hooked on alcohol and other drugs on purpose. Help us to be strong.

Peer pressure is very hard to run from at this age.

We know there need to be rules. Hold us accountable to keep them, and we will.

When our friends drop out of school, sometimes it's almost as if you're glad they do.

When our parents stay away, often it's because they don't trust us or feel needed.

Sometimes, the adults here are rude.

Sometimes, the adults here are not good role models for us.

Sometimes, adults can practice verbal and emotional abuse on students.

School should be the safest, coolest, most inspiring oasis, as we too swiftly grow up.

School must always be a place where everyone knows your name.

Staff would quite possibly share ideas such as:

Trust us and let us share our expertise with our students.

Empower and equip us—hold us accountable to be great teachers.

Care for us as persons first—not as objects on your assembly line of production.

Give us time and space to provide a pleasant classroom environment for our students.

Turn us loose. How can we bottle up knowledge and truly be effective?

Give us resources. We need tools and people for the specific needs of every student.

Don't load us down with paperwork.

When we meet, can we work as teams to find better answers and not gripe?

Please don't talk down to us, or impose ridiculous rules that are irrelevant to learning.

Please never ask us to show political favoritism to a child.

Please never get us in a parent conference and then waffle on school policies.

We believe in grace. Help us as a school to be about grace.

We believe in relationships. Help us as staff members to be relentless about relationships.

Tell us what we're doing well. We need to hear you have noticed.

Tell us what areas we need to develop further, and help us to keep growing.

Don't allow a toxic, gossipy, distrustful culture to poison this school. Do something.

When our school plays favorites, it really hurts the entire staff, students, and community.

We believe we can have a great school for this community—for every student and family.

Help us chart the course. Help us with a bold vision.

You see, the kids know. And the staff knows. After all, they are the ones in the trenches building community every day. They will always have the best vantage point to lead us down a path to greatness and unparalleled effectiveness as local community schools. Always, if we will but listen.

QUESTIONS FOR REFLECTION

1. What key changes would you recommend for your school to go from good to great?
2. Does your school encourage exchange of ideas between the student body and staff on a regular basis?

3. What is the most exciting attribute of your school's culture and total menu of services?
4. What "walls" are obstructing your school from being creative, free, and unchained?

SUGGESTIONS FOR FURTHER READING:

Collins, J. (2001). *Good to Great.* New York: HarperBusiness.
Glaser, J. (2007). *Creating We.* Avon, MA: Platinum Press.

References

Armstrong, T. (1998). *Awakening Genius in the Classroom*. Alexandria, VA: Association for Supervision and Curriculum Development.

Asim, J. (2007). *The N Word: Who Can Say It, Who Shouldn't, and Why*. Boston: Houghton. Mifflin.

Blanchard, K., P. Zigarmi, and D. Zigarmi (1985). *Leadership and the One Minute Manager*. New York: William Morrow and Company, Inc.

Blankstein, A. (2004). *Failure is Not an Option: Six Principles That Guide Student Achievement in High Performing Schools*. Thousand Oaks, CA: Corwin Press and the Hope Foundation.

Bukatko, D., and M. W. Daehler (2004). *Child Development: A Thematic Approach* (5th edition). Boston: Houghton Mifflin.

Citrin, J., and R. Smith (2003). *The 5 Patterns of Extraordinary Careers*. New York: Crown Business.

Clare, E. (2003). *Digging Deep: Thinking about Privilege*. Retrieved February 3, 2010, from http://eliclare.com/what-eli-offers/lectures/privilege.

Coleman, J. (1966). *The James Coleman Report*. Boston: Harvard University.

Collins, J. (2001). *Good to Great*. New York: HarperBusiness.

Covey, S. (2004) *The 7 habits of highly effective people*. New York: Free Press.

Diebert, J. P., and W. K. Hoy (1977). Custodial High Schools and Self-Actualization of Students. *Educational Research Quarterly*, 2(2) (Summer 1977), 21–34.

DuFour, R., R. Eaker, and G. Karhanck (2002). *Whatever It Takes—How Professional Learning Communities Respond When Kids Don't Learn*. Bloomington, IN: National Educational Services.

Edmonds, Ronald R. (1981). Making Schools Effective. *Social Policy*, 12(2) (September–October 1981), 56–61.

———. (1979) Some Schools Work and More Can. *Social Policy*, 9(5) (March–April), 29–32.

Espinosa, L. (2004). Exploring race relations. *Rethinking Schools Online,* 18(3). Retrieved February 3, 2010, from http://www.rethinkingschools.org/archive/18_03/expl183.shtml.

Fleming, N. L. (1980). *A Study of the Relationship between Student Perception of the Organizational Climate of the Schools and Student Achievement.* Utah State University. Dissertation Abstracts International, Vol. 41/10-A, 1980.

Gardner, H. (2006). *Five Minds for the Future.* Boston: Harvard Business School Press.

Garlow, J. (2002). *The 21 Irrefutable Laws of Leadership—Tested by Time.* Nashville: Thomas Nelson.

Gay, G., and J. A. Banks (2000). Culturally Responsive Teaching: Theory, Research, and Practice. *Multicultural Education Series,* No. 8. Teachers College Press.

Gladwell, M. (2008). *Outliers—The Story of Success.* New York: Little, Brown, and Company.

Glaser, J. (2007). *Creating We.* Avon, MA: Platinum Press.

Goodlad, J. I. (1979). *What Schools Are For.* Bloomington, IN: Phi Delta Kappan Educational Foundation.

Guskey, T. (1985). *Implementing Mastery Learning.* Belmont, CA: Wadsworth Publishing.

Green, R. L. (2010). *The Four Dimensions of Principal Leadership.* Boston: Allyn & Bacon.

Gurian, M. (2001). *Boys and Girls Learn Differently: A Guide for Teachers and Parents.* San Francisco: Jossey-Bass.

Hartley, M., and W. K. Hoy (1972). Openness of School Climate and Alienation of High School Students. *Journal of Educational Research,* 23 (1972), 17–24.

Hatch, D., and S. Covey (2006). *Everyday Greatness.* Nashville: Rutledge Hill Press.

Hoxby, C. (2003). *National School Board Meeting Presentation.* San Francisco.

Hughes, R. (2003). *The Educational Good News for Hardin County Schools.* (A compilation of research for district use). Elizabethtown, KY: Hardin County Schools.

Jenkins, W. (2004). *Understanding and Educating African American Children—Excuses to Excellence.* St. Louis, MO: William Jenkins Enterprise.

Johnson, R. (2002). *Using Data to Close the Achievement Gaps: How to Measure Equity in Our Schools.* Thousand Oaks, CA: Corwin Press Inc.

Kidder, R. (1995). *How Good People Make Tough Choices: Resolving the Dilemmas of Ethical Living.* New York: Fireside.

Kirby, P., L. Paradise, and R. Protti (1990, April). *The Ethical Reasoning of School Administrators: The Principled Principal.* Paper presented at the 1990 annual meeting of the AERA. Full text retrieved February 3, 2010, from http://www.eric.ed.gov/ERICDocs/data/ericdocs2sql/content_storage_01/0000019b/80/20/74/19.pdf.

Kolb, D. A., I. M. Rubin, and J. M. McIntyre (1985). *Organizational Psychology: A Book of Readings.* Chicago: The Dorsey Press.

Kohn, A. (1999). *The Schools Our Children Deserve.* New York: Houghton Mifflin Company.

Ladson-Billings, G. (1997). *The Dreamkeepers: Successful Teachers of African American Children.* San Francisco: Jossey-Bass.

Marshall, C., and M. Olivia (2010). *Leadership for Social Justice—Making Revolutions in Education.* Boston: Allyn & Bacon.

Marzano, R. (2002). *What Works in Schools—Translating Research into Action.* Alexandria, VA: Association for Supervision and Curriculum Development.

Maxwell, J. C. (2010). *Everyone Communicates—Few Connect.* Nashville: Thomas Nelson.

McCook, J. E. (2006). *The RTI Guide: Developing and Implementing a Model in Your Schools.* Atlanta: LRP Publications.

Middleton, K., and E. Pettit (2007). *Who Cares?* Tucson, AZ: Wheatmark.

Orwell, G. (1954). *Animal Farm.* New York: Harcourt Brace.

Palmer, P. (1993). *To Know As We Are Known.* New York: HarperOne.

Patterson, K., J. Grenny, R. McMillan, and A. Switzler (2002). *Crucial Conversations: Tools for Talking When Stakes Are High.* Columbus, OH: McGraw Hill.

Payne, R. (1996). *Framework for Understanding Poverty.* Highlands, TX: Aha Process, Inc.

Raiche, J. J., editor (1983). *School Improvement—Research-Based Components and Processes for Effective Schools.* Minnesota: Educational Cooperative Service Unit of the Metropolitan Twin Cities Area.

Richeson, J., and Nussbaum, R. (2004). The Impact of Multiculturalism versus Color-Blindness on Racial Bias. *Journal of Experimental Social Psychology,* 40(3), 417–423.

Senge, P., N. Cambron-McCabe, T. Lucas, B. Smith, J. Dutton, and A. Kleiner (2000). *Schools That Learn: A Fifth Discipline Fieldbook for Educators, Parents and Everyone Who Cares about Education.* New York: Doubleday.

Sergiovanni, T. J. (2005). *Strengthening the Heartbeat.* San Francisco: Jossey-Bass.

Shapiro, J., and J. Stefkovich (2005). *Ethical Leadership and Decision Making in Education: Applying Theoretical Perspectives to Complex Dilemmas.* Mahwah, NJ: Lawrence Erlbaum Associates, Inc.

Silver, H., R. Strong, and M. Perini (2000). *So Each May Learn—Integrating Learning Styles and Multiple Intelligences.* Alexandria, VA: Association for Supervision and Curriculum Development.

Skiba, R., R. Michael, A. Nardo, and R. Peterson (2002). The Color of Discipline: Sources of Racial and Gender Disproportionality in School Punishment. *The Urban Review,* 34(4), 317–342.

Slocumb, P., and R. Payne (2000). *Removing the Mask: Giftedness in Poverty.* Highlands, TX: Aha Process, Inc.

Sousa, D. (2001). *How the Special Needs Brain Learns.* Thousand Oaks, CA: Corwin Press Inc.

Tomlinson, C. (2001). *How to Differentiate Instruction in Mixed Ability Classrooms.* Upper Saddle River, NJ: Prentice Hall.

Tushman, M. L., and C. A. O'Reilly III (2002). *Winning through Innovation.* Boston: Harvard Business School Press.

Wallace, R. (2009). *Breaking Away from the Corporate Model—Even More Lessons from Principal to Principal.* Lanham, MD: Rowman & Littlefield Education.

———. *The Servant Leader and High School Change—More Lessons from Principal to Principal.* Lanham, MD: Rowman & Littlefield Education.

Williams, B. (2003). *Closing the Achievement Gap.* Alexandria, VA: Association for Supervision and Curriculum Development.

About the Authors

David Barnett is chair of the Department of Foundations and Graduate Studies in Education at Morehead State University (MSU). He joined the faculty at MSU in 2002, after serving for more than 27 years in four school districts as middle school teacher, instructional supervisor, federal programs coordinator, finance officer, assistant superintendent, and superintendent. He earned his doctorate in educational administration and supervision from the University of Kentucky in 1986.

Richard Hughes, whose career in public education began in 1968, retired in 2006, after having served as principal in three large Kentucky high schools and superintendent in two school districts. Since that time, he has been a full-time instructor, teaching school leadership courses for Morehead State University. His career includes seven years in private business (as owner of a farm supply and home hardware center), two years in the army, and a tour of duty in Vietnam. In 1986, he earned his doctorate in educational administration from the University of Kentucky.

Rocky Wallace is a full-time instructor at Morehead State University and a former principal of a U.S. Blue Ribbon School in Kentucky. He has served at the Kentucky Department of Education as a leadership consultant to principals, and at the Kentucky Educational Development Corporation as the director of instructional support. He completed his doctorate in strategic leadership from Regent University in 2007, and he has authored a series of principal mentoring books that illustrate the core values of servant leadership.

Carol Christian is a district achievement gap coordinator with the Kentucky Department of Education. She is an adjunct professor, completing her doctorate at the University of Louisville. Her educational journey includes working as a K–12 physical education teacher, a middle school principal, and an author. She was selected to serve Kentucky in the Highly Skilled Educator Program, working with district and school leadership to build leadership capacity to improve student achievement.